SELF-PROMOTION WITHOUT SOCIAL MEDIA

33 Ways to Get Seen, Feel Connected, and Grow Your Business

CREATIVE MINDS
creativemindshq.com

A catalogue record for this book is available from the
National Library of Australia at catalogue.nla.gov.au

Book design by Tess McCabe
www.tessmccabe.com.au

Author photo by Martina Gemmola
www.gemmola.com

All web addresses are current at time of writing.

ISBN 978-0-9946273-9-1 (paperback)
ISBN 978-0-6458449-0-0 (ePub)

DISCLAIMER
The information provided in this book is for educational purposes only and is
general in nature. It is not tailored or customised to a particular business or
industry niche. The author/publisher makes no guarantee of financial results
obtained by using this book and is not liable or responsible for any loss,
damage, or variations between expectation and outcome allegedly arising
from any suggestion or information contained in this book.

SPECIAL THANKS
This book was made possible in part via support from
Creative Victoria and Regional Arts Victoria.

This book was written and designed on Wurundjeri Woi-wurrung country. I use and benefit from First Nations' land that was never ceded, so I make a monthly donation to Pay The Rent. Pay The Rent is 'a grassroots-to-grassroots initiative; it enables funds to be contributed by individuals directly to grassroots causes and campaigns with a focus on protecting First Nations rights, and [offering] practical support'.

Contents

ACTIVITY KEY: ✸ Quick win!   ◎ Recommended for brand-new businesses

✧ Leverage your social media community/content   ⁕ Slow-burn (with good return!)

How to make the most of this book

This book is designed to be a practical resource that you will use and return to at different stages in the life of your business.

I encourage you to write, draw, mark, scribble, highlight, and fold corners.

Think of it as a notebook — a place to sketch out plans, make lists, and be creative.

Make it your own!

GLOSSARY OF TERMS

Topics like digital marketing, website design, search engine optimisation (SEO) and graphic design can feel rife with industry jargon. Check out the Resources and Recommendations blog below for a useful glossary of terms.

RESOURCES AND RECOMMENDATIONS BLOG

I love recommending tools and sharing inspiring resources that help business owners turn their self-promotion plans into reality. Rather than commit only a short list to these printed pages, I've started a blog for you!

Visit **www.creativemindshq.com/spwsm** and enter the password **spwsm** for access.

Throughout this book I'll dive into different self-promotion activities and the reasons to explore them in your own business.

Look out for these icons.

TIPS AND IDEAS

Advice and strategies for finding success with a self-promotion activity

DOUBLE DUTY

Notes on how one activity could be repurposed or lead to another

ACTION

Get your creative juices flowing and plan how to promote your business

REMEMBER

Things to remember as you build your self-promotion muscle

QUICK CHAT

Interviews with business owners who have found success with different self-promotion activities

DECIDING WHAT (AND WHAT NOT) TO FOCUS ON

Self-promotion can feel daunting whether you're starting a brand new business or have been running one for years. No matter what stage you're at, I've categorised the activities on the Contents (page iv) to help you decide where to focus your time, energy, and resources:

* ✳ Quick win!
* ◎ Recommended for brand-new businesses
* ✧ Leverage your existing social media community/content
* ⁂ Slow-burn (with good return!)

You can also mark these checkboxes in the sidebar next to each activity:

☐ YES, DO IT!
☐ SOMETHING TO CONSIDER
☐ NOT APPLICABLE

Feeling overwhelmed?
Start small.
Use the goal setting
worksheet on page 114
to decide where you'll
focus your energy.

Introduction

LESS SOCIALS, MORE CONNECTIONS

There are a lot of different businesses in the world, and lots of advice for marketing those businesses to the masses.

But one portion of the small business economy often overlooked is the micro-businesses: the companies of one. Call us solopreneurs or freelancers, we are the artists, entrepreneurs, designers, writers, consultants, illustrators, coaches, retailers, musicians, educators, filmmakers, architects, stylists, editors, craftspeople, directors, online business managers, and a host of other professionals that just don't have the capacity to employ a marketing and communications team. We wear many hats. We are often emotionally invested in our work in a way that employees are not. We have a vocation, a desire to express something within ourselves and share our talents with the world.

If you think back to the businesses you buy from and the service providers you have worked with, you have probably chosen them based on likeability, trustworthiness, or their visibility. The Know, Like, Trust marketing concept is a framework that businesses use to build relationships with their customers. It involves creating awareness about your services or products (Know), creating a positive image of your business (Like), and establishing credibility and reliability with potential customers and clients (Trust). For many business owners — and especially solo business owners — marketing with this framework in mind should be a priority.

Social media can be an effective self-promotion activity, and for some businesses and self-employed people, it's worth putting lots of time and effort into. On a platform where the main idea is to frequently share images, text, and video about yourself, it can seem all too easy for people to get to know you, to like you, and to trust you.

However, devoting time and effort to social media content creation shouldn't come at the expense of other activities that could also establish connections with your ideal customers and clients. Social media is not inherently good or bad, it just is. It's a space we have little control over as users, and only slightly more control if we pay a platform to show people our content. Over the last decade, we have adapted our lives and businesses to suit social media's very limited format. While true human-to-human connections can be made, they are conditional. Conditional on always giving more time, more effort, more creativity, with diminishing returns.

Undeniably, social media platforms can also be unsafe spaces where people face bullying, trolling and vilification because of their race, gender expression, sexuality, or religion. Promoting a business on platforms where you are vulnerable to abuse can have severe effects on mental and emotional health. Disturbingly, online platforms seem to tolerate bad behaviour — and it's easy to guess why.

If you've picked up this book, it's possible you have noticed your customers and clients are changing their relationship to social media. Your relationship with it as a personal or business user probably has too. This might look like:

- following fewer people, or changing the types of people and brands that you follow
- engaging less and creating less content for the platform
- checking in much less frequently, when once your social media use was daily (or many times a day!); and/or
- feeling like you're putting a lot of effort into creating content, but not getting much in return.

I definitely feel this way, and through a combination of conversation and observation, I know most of my clients and customers have changed their social media habits too. Knowing and understanding the audience for your services and products is crucial to the success of your business, and any self-promotion activity. You should be strive to understand where, and how, they 'hang out' online, just as you should know how your product or service fits in to their lives, what other similar businesses they engage with, as well as what delights and what frustrates them. Getting to know your audience involves intuition, listening, and empathy in addition to hard data and analytics. Committing to always learning about your ideal client or customer will not only help you to target your self-promotion activities, but will result in them seeing you as likeable and trustworthy, too.

THINK OUTSIDE THE SOCIAL MEDIA SQUARE

Now that social media platforms are in their teen years, some days it can feel like we have forgotten about all the ways we used to promote our businesses and our work before digital media entered our lives.

The inspiration for writing this book came from my own needs and desires, and those I saw as the needs of my clients. The wish to invest in other forms of connection, visibility, and promotion — avenues that don't have to conform with social media's ever-changing parameters.

This book is a set of prompts, ideas, tips and invocations. It's not a to-do list, or a strict methodology for self-promotion. It's an opportunity to get offline and start thinking more strategically, and creatively, about how to promote your business. I don't expect you to invest time in everything I suggest in the book, and in fact, even I don't do all these things all the time to promote my own business. I choose what I feel works, what feels right, what feels enjoyable, and what I can feasibly dedicate my time to. I try, I experiment, learn and evolve.

Choose some, not all. Invest your time in those that will have a decent return in terms of visibility. Some might not be relevant or even applicable to your industry or audience. Experiment with new ways to engage with customers or clients (especially if it feels like you're always talking to the same people on social media, or your business has reached a plateau). But above all, don't get discouraged if nothing seems like it's 'working'. Being in business (and marketing yourself) is often a long-game strategy, and you can't conjure or measure success overnight. Experimentation is key.

You may still need to create 'content', but unlike social media content, it can be more targeted, and less ephemeral. You can be you, and you can break free of homogeneity. Different forms of content—depending on the way it is delivered—can live longer and work harder for you and your business. Some may resonate more strongly with your audience than a social media post ever will. You might have fewer connections with customers and clients, but they will be stronger and will build a more sustainable business over time.

As a business owner, you can't just wait for promotional opportunities to tap you on the shoulder. In the world outside of social media, you're in the driver's seat, and you can choose how to get your name out there.

WHO AM I?

I've been sustainably self-employed for most of my career (two decades and counting!). And by sustainably, I mean that I have had a steady stream of income, clients (both new and returning), book sales, and projects that make me feel comfortable financially and fulfilled creatively. My business is a mix of services (design for small businesses) and products (books and resources for creative professionals). There have been periods where I have wound back my service-based projects and focused more on selling products, and vice-versa.

My business and reputation has been built steadily through a series of self-promotional activities that aren't focused on cultivating a large social media following. I believe marketing and self-promotion is a long-game strategy of visibility: across platforms, mediums, and in front of different audiences.

For a few years, I was a digital marketing manager in a small business. Across that relatively short time, the social media landscape changed dramatically. Algorithms started to take hold, followers were harder to gain and retain, and the expectation of content quality skyrocketed. It was 24/7, every day of the year.

When I started to focus on my own business full time again, I couldn't fathom creating social media content to promote myself. I was also having conversations with clients, colleagues and friends about the drain of social media — the algorithm, skewed metrics, excessive advertising costs, and argumentative commenters. So I concentrated on other self-promotion activities that felt more natural to me, like designing a great website, creating educational resources, doing talks and workshops, and sending an email newsletter. I soon found a steady flow of clients engaging me for the kind of design work I loved doing, and it made me think more broadly about how many opportunities there are to market a business — and connect with customers and clients — outside of the social media algorithm.

When I work with my clients on their visual identity design, website design, or book design, we frequently discuss marketing and promotion. We talk about their long- and short-term goals, and how different self-promotion activities can drive towards that destination. Thus, most of the design decisions I make in our work together are in service of these goals. I am designing or setting up systems that help them get there.

This book is an extension of those conversations, activities, and ideas. I share my experience with activities that I have tried before along the way, and I've interviewed seven fellow business owners to share their wisdom too. And you know what? I'm going to be using this book in the same way you are — to help me step away from the screen, brainstorm, and be inspired to promote my business in different and creative ways.

TO BE, OR NOT TO BE, ON SOCIAL MEDIA

Self-promotion can be an exhausting prospect for people who identify as an introvert — their energy is depleted, rather than replenished, by interactions with others. I get it — I am one! Like architect Yvonne Meng (whose interview you can read on page 52), it takes a lot of mental and emotional effort for me to 'toot my own horn'. I find that a lot of self-employed people are introverted, or ambiverts. (We like to spend time alone. I guess that's why we opt to be *sole* traders).

My relationship to social media, especially as it relates to my business, is complicated. I've been 'on' social media since almost the beginning. My own social media accounts still exist, but in terms of being regularly fed with content, they are largely dormant. I consider them an extension of my website: an archive of my work, thoughts, and activities. They exist as a way for *other* people on those platforms to find and promote my work. I don't have a regular social media content-posting strategy. I certainly find some social media platforms useful: as a messaging portal; as a place to learn about what drives and delights my ideal customers and clients; and for self-education, finding support, and sharing recommendations.

So, I'm certainly not advocating that you delete your accounts (as tempting as it can be some days). Having a presence on social media platforms for your business can actually be a great way to get *off* the hamster wheel of social media self-promotion. If you are starting a brand new business, a social media presence might be worth concentrating on in the early days, especially if you know your audience congregates on one platform or another. But by expanding your reach across other activities, you can take healthy breaks, go at a slower pace, and avoid the eventual burnout and resentment the hamster wheel of social media self-promotion can bring.

Like most of us, I'm not immune to envy or self-doubt, especially when it comes to my peers' well-curated, popular feeds that are always brimming with fresh content. So, I have set up systems for myself to reduce the guilt-inducing time-suck those apps can be. I've learned to measure success by how I feel, each and every day, in my business. And I feel good about not relying solely on social media for my self-promotion.

I have used many of the activities I talk about in this book to promote my own businesses over the years. And I have helped my clients — who range from sole traders to businesses and organisations with employees and teams — to implement or build up marketing ideas outside of social media promotion.

INCOME STREAM VS SELF-PROMOTION OPPORTUNITY

Some of the suggestions in this book may be of interest to you because they are a way to bring an additional income stream into your business.

Late-stage capitalism will have us believe that everything can and should be monetised — and is a failure if it doesn't turn a profit. While investigating multiple revenue streams is important for any small or solo business, this guide will focus mainly on activities that will increase your visibility, in order to attract the right customers and clients to your primary service or product base.

Many of these self-promotion activities come with non-monetary, but still valuable benefits, such as meeting professional peers, learning new skills, or pursuing a long-held idea to fruition. All of these outcomes make for a more enjoyable business and life, and making additional revenue is a nice bonus.

NOTHING VENTURED, NOTHING GAINED

One of my favourite sayings in business (and life) is 'nothing ventured, nothing gained'. What benefit is forgone if you choose to rely only on social media promotion at the expense of other avenues?

As you read through these pages of ideas, underline those that resonate. Jot ideas in the margins. You will feel bubbles of excitement as you consider the possibilities for your business. But I won't lie: **you might also feel a bit overwhelmed**. So, start small. Look for 'quick wins', like improving your email signature (page 2), or finding an event to attend (page 42). No effort is wasted if it gets you thinking, moving, doing, or learning.

My hope is that as you find yourself spending less time on the endless treadmill of content posting, scrolling, and counting likes, you have more time for the more enriching parts of your business, your craft, and your life.

Now — separate yourself from the screen.

Grab your favourite beverage, sharpen a pencil, and find a comfy place to sit.

This could be the start of something beautiful.

Repurposing content

If you have come to this book having spent time promoting your business mostly through social media, it can feel overwhelming when you choose to step back or try different self-promotion activities. But all the effort you have put into building and maintaining a social media audience, and creating content for those platforms, need not go to waste. Likewise, new businesses can make content go further, faster with these ideas.

IF YOU HAVE...	
High quality photos & images	**Popular social media posts**
• Make them a focus of your website (page 8) • Get them on Pinterest to send traffic to your website (page 63) • Add them to awards applications (page 107) • Add them to member directories (page 18) • Produce printed collateral that people want to keep (page 64)	• Create educational content on that topic and add it to your website (page 8) • Talk more about that topic on a podcast (page 85) • Co-create a product or service for a relevant charity (page 48) • Add it to Pinterest to send traffic to your website (page 63)
Educational content	**A strong social media community**
• Create a lead magnet to entice newsletter subscribers (page 12) • Make it into newsletter content (page 36) • Host a podcast mini-series (page 85) • Hold a workshop (page 93) • Create evergreen video content (page 54) • Host a panel event or talk (page 45) • Increase your visibility amongst your peers (page 21) • Self-publish a book (page 96) • Add it to your website (page 8) • Pursue guest blogging opportunities that will link back to your website (page 15)	• Start asking for reviews (page 4) • Pitch a collaboration (page 78) • Hold workshops or demonstrations (page 93) • Start a podcast (page 85) • Improve your customer or client experience (page 28) • Reward them (page 81) • Create merchandise (page 101)

⚡

The terms marketing and self-promotion can feel icky sometimes — like promoting our business is somehow 'tricking' people into parting with their money. Let's reframe those concepts. Circle the terms that resonate with you...

Increasing your visibility

Making and maintaining connections

Finding a valued-aligned audience

Helping people to Know, Like and Trust you

Nourishing community

Rewarding loyalty

Generating word of mouth

Championing your industry

Providing value

Helping people

Strengthening ties

Generating referrals

Cultivating community

Relationship building

Finding your people

Introducing yourself

Getting more 'right fit' enquiries

Add your own:

1 _____

2 _____

3 _____

1

Improve your email signature

I'm always a little curious when a customer or newsletter subscriber has a domain name email address. Who doesn't love a little internet sleuthing? I have signed up to events, lists, or even made dinner reservations using my tess@tessmccabe.com.au email address, only to have the business contact me later and become a client. Clearly, they were doing some internet sleuthing of their own.

Think about how many emails you send out in a day, a week, a month or a year. What would happen if each of those people clicked through to your website? Not only would it increase your website traffic, it could potentially turn that person into a new customer or client.

TIPS AND IDEAS

- Don't make your email signature a flat image. Clickable links (especially one to your website) is best.

- Align your email signature with your business' visual identity. It should, at the very least, include your logo or main brand colours.

- You may not be able to include your exact brand font in your email signature, as some fonts are not email-safe and won't be correctly displayed in all email platforms and browsers. Choose a standard serif or sans-serif and let colour, your logo or other graphics connect your email signature to the visual identity of your website or marketing collateral.

- Consider adding a section where you can announce or promote a current piece of content, a service or product. This can be changed regularly so frequent receivers of your emails are learning something new about you in a subtle way.

- Use an email signature builder or platform to style your email signature — the Resources and Recommendations blog has some examples (see page 113).

ACTION

☐ To ensure uniformity, set up a document listing the Hex and RGB colour codes used in your visual branding. Keep the document handy so you can refer to them quickly as needed and so you can share with designers and collaborators. See page 62 for a template.

☐ You'll have limited options in terms of typefaces that can display uniformly on all your email recipient's devices. System fonts or web-safe fonts are recommended. Decide whether a serif or sans-serif typeface suits your business' visual identity better or choose from the following:

- Sans-serif: Arial/Helvetica, Verdana, Tahoma, or Trebuchet
- Serif: Times New Roman, Georgia, or Courier New

☐ Send yourself or some close friends some test emails (from desktop and mobile) and check that links are clickable, and that everything formats correctly.

☐ Add your email signature to your preferred email platform.

☐ Make versions of the email signature for staff or other email accounts as needed, to ensure a uniform look across all your email communications.

☐ NOT APPLICABLE   ☐ SOMETHING TO CONSIDER   ☐ YES, DO IT!

```
{ 2 }
```

Ask for reviews

Reviews, testimonials and recommendations are a powerful promotion tool because they can help to build trust and credibility — it's the social proof that you can and will do what your other marketing says. Reviews are often sought out by people who are considering a purchase, which is one step closer than 'just browsing'.

Reviews collected on platforms like Google will likely help your SEO too. While I don't have a huge number of client reviews on my own profile, my website enquiry rate has vastly improved since I asked clients to review me directly on Google.

 TIPS AND IDEAS

◆ People who look to reviews are often looking for third-party proof that what you say in your own marketing and promotion is true, and that the experiences of those who have used your product or service before mirrors what they want. So supply your clients and customers with suggestions for specific details they could include in their review, that will help them share insights that others might find useful.

◆ When requesting a review, make it easy by providing ideas for what your customer or client can write — this will help your reviews highlight the special skills or features that make your business different.

◆ Create a template or automated email that you can send out after a customer or client has used your service or purchased your product. Automate it, or make it easy to send quickly (so you don't get nervous and not send it at all!).

◆ Reply to reviews, if the platform allows it. Not only is it a courtesy to the client or customer who has reviewed you, it shows a greater level of care. It also gives readers context if the review highlights any issues regarding your product or service that might be deemed negative.

- Consider whether your customers will be discerning regarding the verification of reviews as coming from actual customers. Many online apps will offer a verification that the person who is commenting has actually purchased your product.

- If you're just starting your business, reach out to past colleagues for testimonials or consider offering complimentary services or products in exchange for a review.

- Businesses that sell products (and have lots of customers) could consider adding an incentive such as a random prize draw for anyone who leaves a review in a given time period.

- Give reviews to your suppliers, those who support your business, and other businesses and services you use — especially those that you have had a genuinely good experience with. Karma, baby.

🔋 DOUBLE DUTY

- Add customer reviews to your website (page 8) or printed marketing collateral (page 64).

- Set up a Google Business Profile to gather reviews, it may help your search engine optimisation (page 7).

☀ ACTION

List where you would like to collect reviews based on where you think the majority of customers would likely find you, or where they would be considering a purchase.

_____

_____

_____

_____

_____

_____

Write your template or automated email — you might have a few variations based on the type of interaction your customers have with you. Include links to the places people can leave you a review — this will lower the barrier for customers and clients to leave good feedback.

_____

_____

_____

_____

_____

_____

_____

_____

_____

_____

_____

_____

_____

_____

_____

_____

_____

_____

_____

☐ Now add these templates into your email client or shortcut program, or add it to a post-purchase email sequence.

3

THE POWER OF A GOOGLE
BUSINESS PROFILE

Google is the world's biggest search engine, and it's difficult to deny its impact on the promotion of businesses through tools like Google Maps and Google Reviews. Even if your business does not have a physical location, creating a Google Business profile and adding your general location (neighbourhood or city) can help potential customers find you. If you sell products online, you can add them to Google Merchant Center to make them more visible in search results.

Google knows where people are, so by telling them the physical headquarters of your business, your website will start appearing in search results for customers located in that city or region. While this might be perfect if you're a local business that aims to serve the local community, it could be less ideal if you're an online business that can help customers regardless of their location. Regardless, being transparent about your business' location will build trust with a potential customer.

If you're planning to move to a new city, activating your Google Business Profile can help you build up your local search results before you even set up in your new location. This means that when you do set up shop, you'll already have a presence on Google and be easier for potential customers to find.

Once you've activated your Google Business Profile, you can start gathering Google Reviews. These reviews can appear on the search engine results page and can convince potential visitors of the value of your products or services before they've even clicked through to your website. And the more positive, 5-star reviews you receive, the more Google will register that your website is one that visitors like and trust.

☐ NOT APPLICABLE ☐ SOMETHING TO CONSIDER ☐ YES, DO IT!

{4}

Optimise your website (for search engines and humans)

Having a website that is optimised for both search engines and your website visitors can go a long way in attracting your ideal customers and clients.

When someone visits your website, you want to make sure their query is answered. This 'query' will be different for every business. It could be as broad as 'what, or who, is this website about?', or as specific as 'will this artist paint my pet's portrait?'.

You want to portray authenticity and trustworthiness through your website — it's a great start to having people like, know and trust you.

If your website visitors are interested and engaged, they're more likely to stay on and explore your website and — ideally — take action.

💡 TIPS AND IDEAS

◆ Don't make visitors hunt for key information on your website. Include things like contact information, opening hours or a list of services in multiple locations. Identify your navigation with words like 'Shop', 'Services', 'Contact', and 'About'.

◆ If a casual visitor finds your website through a list of search engine results, ideally they'll discover a homepage that features:

- A statement about what your business does, who it's for, and what problem it solves for them
- Images that illustrate your services, products, or outcomes for your clients and customers
- Easily digestible text in short paragraphs
- Reviews or testimonials
- Helpful resources, such as snippets of blog posts
- Calls to action in more than one place. For example, how to contact you, where to buy etc.

- Build trust by making it clear who is behind the business. You don't have to share every intimate detail, but you do have to be visible in some way. What might this look like? E.g.:

  - A high quality photo of yourself
  - Information about why you do what you do
  - Some background about how you got to this point
  - Contact details that are easy to find.

- Improve the accessibility of your website design and content. There are a number of simple ways to make your website accessible and inclusive for people of all abilities:

  - Add alt-text descriptions to your images
  - Ensure there is strong contrast between text colour and background colour
  - Make text sizes readable and responsive to magnification on a visitor's browser
  - Use clear, logical website navigation
  - Communicate content clearly and make it 'scannable', through the use of headings, subheadings, captions, bullet points and well-spaced text.

- Ensure your website reformats and resizes elements on different devices including mobile, desktop and tablet.

- Keep image, video and downloadable document sizes small, and install only essential third-party apps.

- Search engines aim to serve up relevant content to users, and relevancy is often tied to timeliness. Set up a regular review schedule for your website, especially to catch any outdated contact information, location details or operating hours. An easy way to ensure your website is regularly updated for new and returning visitors is to start a blog.

- Writing helpful blog content with an SEO-friendly structure can do wonders for your website:

  - It keeps your website regularly updated with fresh content for Google to read, and it tells Google that you have an active business.
  - Blog posts can answer search queries and can offer insight into your business or personality. Both build trust and likeability.
  - Blog posts can become lead magnets (see page 12 for more about lead magnets).
  - Because a blog lives on your website, no matter where you promote it, people will end up on your website.

- Identify your keywords and phrases, and use them naturally in your website content. You'll want to integrate them into:

  - page headings and URLs
  - text content
  - image captions and image descriptions
  - blog posts; and
  - page titles and descriptions.

- Wherever possible, don't duplicate content exactly across different areas of your website. Humans don't respond well to being told the same thing the exact same way over and over, and the SEO robots don't take kindly to it either.

- Customise the search result description and page title for each page, product and blog post on your website.

- Use key words to describe your website's images in their file name before uploading them, and add alt-text descriptions to images. This helps Google Images deliver them to search engine users and also helps your website to be more accessible.

DOUBLE DUTY

- A succinct statement about your business, written for your website's search engine optimisation, can immediately show people how you can help them (page 28).

- Products listed on your website can also be automatically populated as shoppable items on platforms like Google Shopping (page 7) and Pinterest (page 63).

- High-quality backlinks (links to your website from other websites) will improve your website's SEO (page 15). These could be links from interviews or guest blogs on other websites, or a link from a membership directory (page 18).

☼ ACTION

Review your website to ensure it covers off the following at a minimum:

☐ The website menu/navigation is clear and succinct.

☐ It's clear what your business does, who it's for, and what problem it solves for the visitor.

- ☐ The colour of website text across the website has a strong contrast against the background colour.
- ☐ For online shops, there is information about shipping, delivery, returns, sizing, and payment options as applicable.
- ☐ The website has a privacy policy and terms & conditions if it is collecting data through an online shop, mailing list or contact form.
- ☐ It's easy to find information about who is behind the business.
- ☐ There is a clear call to action on every page (e.g. Buy now, Call now, Subscribe here etc).
- ☐ Location and opening hours are clear and easy to find (if applicable).
- ☐ Website looks good and functions properly on desktop and mobile devices.
- ☐ All links and buttons work.
- ☐ Contact details are clear.
- ☐ Contact forms and subscription forms function correctly.
- ☐ The website domain name has a secure https. (Search engines prefer websites with a secure **https** as opposed to simply **http**. On some website platforms, https is free and usually set by default. You might also have the option to 'enable' https via your domain name provider).

Note any updates you want to make below:

_____
_____
_____
_____
_____
_____
_____
_____
_____
_____

(5)

Offer something of value to generate leads

A lead magnet is a marketing tool that helps you build a database of people who are already somewhat invested in you and your business' products or services.

People are wary of handing over their contact details—nobody wants an inbox or letterbox full of junk. So a good lead magnet typically offers something of value to potential customers or clients in exchange for their contact information. Examples of this could include a helpful resource, product samples, templates, discounts, guides and eBooks, demos or trial subscriptions.

I have offered eBooks, educational content, workshops and activities as lead magnets to build my customer mailing list in my own business. Customers usually see the value in staying subscribed to the list if the content is in the same vein as the lead magnet, and through regular contact, they can get to know more about me and the products and services I offer in a way that is not overwhelming.

Lead magnets can also be thought of as a taste of a service or product, or something that the client or customer can have as a first step towards engaging you as a supplier.

 TIPS AND IDEAS

- Your lead magnet can be designed to entice a very specific type of customer. Service providers should ensure they are clear on the type of person you want to attract as a warm lead, and tailor your lead magnet to a specific issue they commonly encounter.

- A person who has already bought something from your business is definitely a warm lead, so consider including a coupon for a future purchase or a promotional code for a discount on their next order. You could also include a small sample of another product from your line, a product that complements the one they purchased, or a catalogue of other products from your business. This not only adds value to the customer's purchase, but also encourages them to shop with you again.

- Other types of lead magnets include educational content like checklists, workbooks, webinars and guides, or membership to a likeminded online community. Here are some ways I've seen businesses use lead magnets:

  - A wedding photographer offers a free guide to posing for engagement photos. It helps couples who want to announce their engagement with beautiful photos. The guide gathers warm leads (recently engaged couples) that could then be offered a photography package.
  - A landscape designer offers a guide to maintaining gardens in different environments and climates.
  - A textile designer with a range of scarves offers an eBook about ways to style the accessory.
  - A jeweller offers a beginners' guide to gemstones and ring styles for people thinking of investing in a custom piece.
  - A coach offers a workbook that helps people to set goals and identify roadblocks, and then nurtures those leads with offers and content that help them to achieve their goals.

▢ DOUBLE DUTY

- Use the lead magnet to entice newsletter signups. Then, encourage subscribers to take the next step through automations that promote your services or product (page 36).
- Repurpose your lead magnet content as a guest post on a third-party website to create in-bound links to your website (see page 15).

☀ ACTION

What is something of value that you can offer to clients that will ultimately help them on their journey to work with or buy from you?

_____

_____

_____

_____

_____

_____

_____

_____

_____

_____

_____

Look at blog posts, social media content, or newsletter content that has gathered the most likes or opens. List themes or topics from this content which could be turned into a lead magnet to make people sign up to your newsletter or engage you for a particular service.

_____

_____

_____

_____

_____

_____

_____

_____

_____

_____

_____

_____

_____

6

THE POWER OF BUILDING INBOUND LINKS TO YOUR WEBSITE

Inbound links (also known as backlinks) from other reputable websites to your website can be incredibly valuable for improving your website's SEO. Search engines like Google see these links as a vote of confidence in your website's authority and value. As a result, websites with more inbound links tend to rank higher in search results.

The benefits of inbound links extend beyond just search engine rankings. When other websites link to your website, they're essentially vouching for your credibility and expertise. This can build trust and recognition with real people who come across your website.

One way to encourage inbound links is to request that a link to your website be added whenever you, your work, or your business is mentioned online. You could even build this into your contract of services to ensure that you're consistently receiving this benefit. Additionally, if you ever offer your services or products as a donation, 'exposure', or at a discounted rate, including a backlink to your website as part of the agreement can provide a simple SEO boost.

In-bound links can also be built through: profiles on membership directories (page 18); interviews or articles on digital media platforms; guest blogs on industry websites; or the websites of your clients or collaborators.

A QUICK CHAT WITH

Elizabeth Bull

PHOTOGRAPHER

I've long admired Liz for two things: her business acumen; and her commitment to work-life harmony. (Actually, make that three things: she also takes beautiful photographs!). Managing both a service-based business and a product line, she also regularly indulges in her love of travel. It's also struck me that a photographer, with a seemingly endless pipeline of imagery to post on social media to promote her businesses, just doesn't. Her early investment in and focus on her websites has been a pipeline for customers and clients.

What's your current vibe re: social media?

Um, nonexistent? Social media doesn't come naturally to me and I don't enjoy it. My most active accounts are really just personal accounts — landscapes that catch my eye, and mark a time or place that I'd like to record. I am more likely to text a small group of friends than broadcast something. [Social media promotion] makes me feel like I am standing on a soap box yelling at no one. Hence, not a strength of mine and not something I've put much effort into working on.

How do the majority of your clients find you?

Through my website and via word of mouth.

Why do you think investing in your website is good for self-promotion and the customer experience?

You own it and you control it. It allows you to bring together and showcase all the information about what you do or sell. Using Google, you can also target people when they are actively searching and ready for your service — compared to Instagram when they are just scrolling. [Social media] of course helps build brand awareness and can connect you with your audience, but is not necessarily when your audience is ready to pull the trigger.

How does your promotion and marketing strategy differ between your service-based business as a photographer, and your product-based business One Fine Print?

My service-based business marketing, other than some networking in the early days, has always been predominantly online. However, I found that some of the more traditional offline marketing strategies were most effective for my product business One Fine Print — pop up shops, events, collaborations, trade shows and even postcards and letter box drops were successful. I think this is because it was a product that translated best when we were physically in front of people.

What are some of the systems and processes you have built in to your business that help to keep your website/s optimised for search engines?

I try to update content regularly. On occasion I've had to review and change the focus of the search engine keywords I even want to rank for. For example, as I've been in the industry a long time, in the time I've been operating some of the keywords people use to search for services like mine have changed. For example, 'headshot' used to mean actor or model headshots, but now people use the term headshot for corporate portraits! Over the years, I've also narrowed down the focus of my business, and subsequently the search engine keywords that I want to focus on.

LIZZYC.COM.AU
ONEFINEPRINT.COM.AU

✦ 7 ✦

Join an online platform with a member directory

Being a part of an industry association can lend credibility to your business or your professional standing within your industry. And depending on the credibility of the industry directory itself, and how long it has had a website presence, your presence on the directory can improve your own website's search engine rankings, making it easier for people to find your website online.

If just one client finds me via a public member directory each year, the annual fees I pay to the industry associations, public directories and membership groups I have joined usually pay for themselves multiple times over. I've also been highlighted by industry associations in the form of interviews, guest blogging opportunities, or features.

Remember that your directory listing may be limited in terms of design and content, so you may not be able to fully showcase your unique brand and its products or services. Consider the directory listing a taste of what clients will find if they click through to your website.

 TIPS AND IDEAS

- Keep your content evergreen and consistent, so you only need to update your listing as needed to reflect significant changes in your business.

- You needn't limit yourself to just associations or guilds related to your specific industry. Seek out supportive networks based around your location or your business' values.

- Depending on your industry, you may be competing with other businesses listed in the same directory, which can make it harder to stand out. Look at the profiles of similar businesses and consider how you can make your unique skills and offers stand out against other providers.

◆ Ask clients or customers where they found you, and check referrals via website analytics, so you can also establish if the directory is working as a promotion tactic.

◆ Don't forget to update these directories if you change your website address, contact details, or any of the major product/service offerings in your business.

🔋🔋 DOUBLE DUTY

◆ Industry associations can help by providing a platform to network with other professionals in the same industry (page 42), access industry-related resources and information, and develop skills and knowledge through training and development opportunities.

◆ Being a member of an association or group can be a lead for things like:

- speaking opportunities at in-person events (page 42)
- collaborations (page 78)
- being seen as an industry leader amongst your peers (page 21); and
- mentoring (page 27).

☀ ACTION

Use a search engine to find industry associations aligned with your service offering or product. Often, industry associations have good SEO so they will pop up within the first few results when searching for a generic term. List the results here:

_____

_____

_____

_____

_____

_____

_____

Check out the websites of industry peers: often people who have accreditations or are members of industry organisations list them on their own websites. List any that are worthy of further investigation here:

_____

_____

_____

_____

_____

Narrow down your list to at least 1, but preferably 2 or 3. Consider annual fees, how many other members offer similar services or products to you.

1 _____

2 _____

3 _____

Itemise what each directory listing features. This will give you a sense of what you need to collate in order to get a profile up.

_____

_____

_____

_____

_____

_____

_____

_____

☐ Lock a time into your calendar to join up and add your profile. Now set a reminder to check your website analytics at 3-month intervals to see if the listing is driving traffic to your website.

8

THE POWER OF VISIBILITY AMONGST YOUR INDUSTRY PEERS

Service providers can often benefit from visibility within their own industry for recommendations and overflow work opportunities. This kind of industry/community can lead to indirect income or a different income source for yourself.

If you're known within your industry as an expert or specialist in a particular task that many can do but not all enjoy, you can benefit from referred work opportunities. Plus, sometimes people just have more work than they can handle—I know from experience that making a trustworthy referral to a potential client always feels better than shutting the door on them.

Ideas to begin increasing your visibility amongst your industry peers include:

- Join a professional body as a member, committee member, or leader.
- Connect with others in your industry through peer support networks, online groups, or industry events.
- Share resources for people in your industry that have worked for you in your business (templates, courses, guides, frameworks, business models etc).
- Promote yourself as an expert in a niche of your industry, through things like industry-related articles, talks, interviews or publicity.
- Put up your hand or pitch yourself for a panels or talks at industry conferences or trade shows.
- Championing people in your industry who are doing good things.

9

Talk about what you do

We've all been in a situation where a conversation has felt like a missed opportunity to give a true picture of yourself. If you're in a position where self-promotion is important to the sustainability of your business (which, let's face it, most solo businesses are!), it's crucial to get comfortable with a succinct description of what you do.

Talking about what you do is not just reserved for networking events. Think about the people you meet when you're on vacation, at a gathering of friends, a school or community function, in a seat on a plane... The question 'what do you do?' is cliche but it's almost as common as talking about the weather.

This tip is something we often hear referred to as 'the elevator pitch'. There are tons of ways to write your pitch but, in my experience, too often they sound like something you would read on a website rather than hear from a person you've just met. They're not written in the way that humans actually talk. The key to describing your business is that if it feels too rehearsed or salesy (or like a pitch!), it can feel unnatural in the context of an incidental conversation. In short, it's a turn-off.

If people are intrigued by what you say, they're more likely to remember you — either as someone they can engage for themselves, or as someone they can recommend to others.

TIPS AND IDEAS

◆ The best interactions happen when you talk about what you do in a way that connects with the listener — their prior knowledge, their interests, the context of the situation: much of this assessment will need to be done on the fly, so becoming confident and fluent in the way you talk about your work makes this a lot easier.

◆ Establish a connection by telling people why you started your business or why you feel called to your profession.

- Good places to practice how you talk about yourself include in the shower, or in your car (basically any glass box where you're alone). You can also record yourself and listen to the recording, looking for areas to improve (I know, this can be excruciating! But no one needs to hear it but you).

- Learn from each interaction and refine how you describe what you do based on the follow-up conversation.

- Offer up just enough information that it gives an accurate picture and doesn't feel like a spiel. You want to encourage follow-up questions.

- Practice speaking confidently about what you do — variations will come naturally when it's time to say it to someone.

⊞ DOUBLE DUTY

- Describing your business succinctly in writing is the backbone of a successful website (page 8).

☀ ACTION

Use the guide below to develop your 'elevator pitch'. We're aiming here for comfort: both for yourself, and for the person you've just met.

How does doing what you do make you feel?

_____

_____

_____

What types of customers or clients do you usually work with?

_____

_____

_____

_____

Do you have any specialised knowledge?

_____

_____

_____

_____

_____

What makes you different from others who also work in your industry or have your profession?

_____

_____

_____

_____

Here are some starter prompts to help you get into 'conversation mode'.

I'm a _____ and I work with people to _____
    (your title/job/business)   *(solve a problem)*

I'm a _____ . Most of my clients are _____ ,
    (your title/job/business)   *(ideal client)*

and I help them _____
                             (solve a problem)

I specialise in _____ for _____ .
    (your specialist area)   *(ideal client or scenario)*

I run a _____ business called _____ . We make
    (specific detail/category)   *(your business name)*

_____ for _____ .
    (describe product)   *(ideal client or scenario)*

It's like: _____ for _____ .
    (a well-known product or service)   *(your ideal client or scenario)*

Think about examples of where your work or business has succeeded or solved a problem for a potential client. Practising how to tell these stories (and making sure the takeaway is working in your favour!) is a good way to talk more specifically about what it's like to work with you.

Example:

_____

_____

_____

Example:

_____

_____

_____

_____

Example:

_____

_____

_____

_____

Write down your 'pitch'. You can also write variations of what you might say based on different service/product offerings, or different social contexts.

_____

_____

_____

_____

_____

_____

_____

☐ Practice saying your pitch out loud. Does it feel weird to say? Say it a few more times (like 10–15 more times). If it's still not sitting right, tweak the above to iron out the wrinkles.

‐⚡‐

It's easy to talk about what you do, and why it is important, when you believe it — but let's be honest: it's hard to get out of your own head sometimes. When you know you have to do some kind of self-promotion thing, get in the mood:

- Listen to your favourite song, the one that makes you sing out loud or dance around.

- Call your best friend (or closest business confidant) and have them tell you why you're so great.

- Read through your 5-star reviews and gushing customer or client emails.

10

THE POWER OF MENTORS

I have been both a mentee and a mentor at different stages across my career, and each relationship I have found helpful for my business. Mentors can provide guidance, support, and advice on how to navigate your career path. They can also share their knowledge and experience, helping you to avoid mistakes and make the most of your opportunities. But crucially, mentors can help you to build your professional network and connect you with other potential clients, customers and collaborators in your field. Mentors can become your cheerleaders, especially if you have worked together to hone and improve your business' offering.

Often, if the mentor has been around in an industry for a long time, they are offered projects and opportunities that they are over-qualified to undertake or no longer align with their professional interests. Plus, they are also asked for recommendations because of their wide networks and standing in the community. This can open up opportunities to receive referrals to contacts you might otherwise not have had access to.

When you enter into a mentoring relationship, you should have some clear goals and outcomes you wish to achieve. But likewise, your mentor should always have a thorough understanding of your career goals and interests, so that any referrals or recommendations they offer will be of benefit to you.

Mentors can come in a variety of shapes and sizes, and it's not always a formal relationship. Look to people you admire: is there someone who has experience and knowledge in your field, and who you feel comfortable asking for guidance and support? The key is to be honest and transparent about your goals and desired outcomes. Not everyone will have the time or inclination to mentor. And not everyone will be willing to spend the time and energy required without the offer of remuneration.

Look for mentorship programs or networking events that offer mentorship opportunities. Joining a professional association could be the first step.

☼ 11 ☼

Improve your customer or client experience

We all know what it's like to have a bad experience parting with hard-earned money. Maybe it's a product or service that didn't meet expectations, or a general sense of confusion or unease when dealing with a business as a customer or client.

For solo and small businesses, a negative customer or client experience in your own business can lead to dissatisfaction, poor reviews, and a damaged reputation. When you run your own business, these interactions can lead to burn-out and contempt ... two things that are sure to extinguish the spark you have for the work you once loved.

A positive customer or client experience is important for all parties involved. In my business, two of the largest drivers of revenue are repeat clients and referred clients — both directly connect to the experience my clients have with me from first enquiry to project delivery, and everything in between. By going the extra mile and providing a positive experience, businesses can increase customer satisfaction and loyalty, which can lead to repeat business and positive word-of-mouth.

☼ TIPS AND IDEAS

◆ Set boundaries and expectations for yourself, and for your clients/customers. This is especially important when your business is just you, and you feel personally connected to each client or customer outcome.

◆ Be clear in communication, and consistent too. Even a quick email with a status update can help to reassure clients and customers that they have your attention and priority. And who doesn't love feeling reassured?

◆ Create a checklist to ensure you're delivering the same quality of service (and customer experience) for each client, regardless of how much they spend. Then, consider how high-ticket or recurring clients or customers could be made to feel extra-valued by working with you.

- Add a thorough FAQ section or ChatBot that can help people feel confident in their purchase.

- Ask for feedback after every client/customer experience, through a public review or private feedback form. This can be important even if a client relationship doesn't extend through the initial enquiry.

- Don't bend over backwards so far that you snap in two! Customer service is relative to each and every business, and every business owner needs to set their own boundaries around how far you will go to ensure 'the customer is always right'. Don't accept bad behaviour, bullying, belittling or blatant disrespect from clients or customers.

 DOUBLE DUTY

- A good customer experience can be ensured by:
  - Optimising your website (page 8).
  - Offering educational content that can help customers and clients get the most out of your product or service (page 12).
  - Designing packaging in such a way that it protects a purchase and delights the customer when they receive it (page 71).

☀ ACTION

Let's look at your current customer experience. Check all that apply.

For service providers:

☐ My website is informative, friendly, and easy to navigate.

☐ There is information about the person that is behind the business (me), including a photo.

☐ Before working with me, I give clients an understanding of my process and an expectation of timelines.

☐ I set expectations around the services I do and don't provide through information on my website, or in conversation.

☐ I have a formal onboard process (e.g. proposal/quote, contract, client portal, welcome document).

☐ I am clear about my terms and conditions or the contractual elements of the relationship with my clients.

☐ I am responsive to email/phone communication.

☐ I deliver on timelines that have been agreed to.

☐ I add value to my core service by helping clients navigate ___ (adjacent need).

☐ I set expectations about my duty to the client after the project is finished.

☐ I empower my clients with guides and resources at different stages of the project

For product sellers:

☐ I provide detailed product information before purchase, including images, size and material details, and video tutorials.

☐ I have an FAQ section that addresses common queries and concerns associated with my product offering.

☐ I am clear with customers about shipping and delivery costs and timelines.

☐ It's clear how customers can pay for their products and that their transactions are secure.

☐ My packaging protects the customer's purchase.

Test your customer experience:

Ask some trusted friends or colleagues to visit your website. What are their first impressions?

_____

_____

_____

_____

_____

_____

_____

What is the overall vibe they receive from your online presence?

_____

_____

_____

_____

Take a friend or colleague through your customer/client journey. Observe their behaviour as they navigate your website and note areas where they are stuck, confused, or need more information.

_____

_____

_____

_____

_____

_____

_____

Note down some ways you can improve or add to your customer experience:

_____

_____

_____

_____

_____

_____

_____

_____

_____

_____

12

Nurture your retailer relationships

Building a successful relationship with your retailers takes time and effort, but the rewards can be significant in terms of increased exposure and sales for your brand.

Marketing to your retailers (and potential wholesale/retail customers) takes a slightly different approach to marketing to a direct customer. You will want to help them sell your product in their store by reminding them about your brand story, the benefits and materials of your product, and assisting them to present your wares in a way that encourages sales.

☀ TIPS AND IDEAS

◆ Help your retailers tell your story by providing them with extra info about collections/products and reinforcing your brand story.

◆ Work with the retailer to create signage and displays that showcase your products in their space. This might be something you customise for each client.

◆ Keep an eye on your retail customer's marketing and communications to their audience. It might give you ideas for how you can help your retailer to promote your business in a way that feels authentic for them.

◆ Offer discounts or promotions for your products within your retailer's store, such as buy-one-get-one-free deals or free samples.

◆ Offer to host in-store events at your retailer's space, such as product launches, demos or workshops, to promote your products and bring new people into their retail space.

◆ Once you have made contact with potential retailers, build the relationship. Provide them with product information, answer their questions, and offer support.

- Keep in touch with your retailers through email, phone, or in-person visits.

- Consider a retailer-only newsletter, marketing material or social media account to provide them with content, media, imagery, or social proof they can use in their own marketing efforts.

- Talking to retailers may help you to understand your customer's needs and develop new product or marketing ideas.

[+|+] DOUBLE DUTY

- Understanding how your products are displayed and found in an environment that you can't control (like a retailer's space) can help you to reinforce or streamline your visual identity and packaging (see pages 58, 64 and 71).

- A retailer may be open to hosting an event such as a product launch, demonstration, or workshop (see pages 45 and 93).

☼ ACTION

Plan a research trip to (or contact) businesses that retail your products. Your aim is to talk to them about their observations of customer interactions with your product, and find out ways you can support them as retailers.

Retailer name & contact details	Date to visit/call/contact

List some ways that the presentation and promotion of your products can be elevated in the context of their store. This could look like presentation options, photography for their online store, a different option for packaging, signage or display furniture.

_____

_____

_____

_____

_____

_____

Talk to your retailer about what they need and their vision for their space. Is there something you can be doing to help them sell more of your product?

_____

_____

_____

_____

_____

_____

_____

_____

Consolidate the ideas or identify some key learnings from your visits or conversations with your retailers.

_____

_____

_____

_____

_____

-⚡-

Structuring and scheduling can reduce the overwhelm that comes with the feeling that you should always be promoting your services (or never seem to be). Just as you likely have a structure around your work hours, implement a structure around how you promote it.

13

Start (or grow) an email newsletter

A newsletter is an effective way to engage with an audience because it means your communication isn't at the behest of an algorithm. Trusting that you acquire those email addresses in an ethical way, your email subscribers are an audience that you manage yourself, and they won't disappear if a social platform shuts down.

Newsletters are designed to reach people in a more personal space—their inbox. As such, you want to honour that interaction as a direct form of conversation. Emails that are all about selling can start to wear on subscribers, leading to less engagement with your message.

I launched my email newsletter, Sylloge, in 2014. The format has remained relatively constant since then—I share a little about my products and services, but mostly I share interesting things I have listened to and read that relate to running a creative business. What I share is coming from a genuine place: I am running a creative business, and for the most part, so is my audience. The value my newsletter provides reflects positively on me as a service-provider and publisher. In theory, if my subscribers consistently like the things I recommend in my newsletter, and see me as a trusted source of informative content, then it's more likely they'll trust that a book I write or publish will be something they want to buy (or they may hire me to design their website or book!).

 TIPS AND IDEAS

- Think about how often you can realistically produce an email newsletter, and stick to that schedule. Like most self-promotion, consistency is key. Set a newsletter schedule that you can reasonably adhere to such as weekly, fortnightly, seasonal. For weekly or fortnightly emails, choose a day and time to send it out, considering your audience and when they might be in a good mental place to open it.

- Think about standardising what you send out, and when, so subscribers know what to expect—you can make this clear on your sign-up form, too.

- If you choose to share a value-based newsletter with an essay, tips/strategies or aggregated content, share links to your products or services sparingly or in a consistent manner.

- If your strategy is to send emails about product releases — and customers sign on for that — add in content about the broader values and benefits of your brand as a secondary message.

- Consider developing an sequence of newsletters with 'evergreen' content that can be automatically sent to a subscriber after they opt-in to your list. This automation might be communication that, over time, describes your services and products in a way that educates your customer, creates positive brand associations, and maintains your visibility in their inbox. I've known business owners who have months of automated newsletter content in place, which takes the pressure off of maintaining a regular newsletter writing and sending schedule.

- It's never too early to start collecting email addresses for a regular newsletter, even if you're not planning to launch one just yet. A short sequence of automated emails sent out after someone opts-in to receive marketing from you can help to build trust and engagement with your business.

- If you have a product-based business, choose a platform that can sync with your online store, and email customers relevant and timely information based on their purchase or browsing behaviour.

- To avoid being caught out by spam laws, make sure you are sending your email newsletter out through a secure platform and that every email includes an 'unsubscribe' link. And if you have an email subscription form on your website, ensure you are covered with an appropriate Privacy Policy and Terms & Conditions.

- To begin building an email list, promote your newsletter (and importantly, the value it offers) on your website, at the end of blog posts, on packaging, in your email signature, or in person (for instance at markets or workshops). You can include 'forward to a friend' links within the newsletter. You might also consider adding a lead magnet that offers something of value to entice subscribers (see page 12).

- Some newsletter platforms offers advantages such as marketing your newsletter to potential subscribers, and making money from your content through paid subscription tiers.

- Remember, you want people on your list who want to be there. Think about that in terms of providing valuable content, and respect those who choose to unsubscribe.

- ◆ Ideas for newsletter content for product-based businesses:

  - Usage, styling or care tips.
  - Behind the scenes of making or designing a product.
  - A 'day in the life' of you/your team.
  - What (or who) is inspiring you to create your products.

- ◆ Ideas for newsletter content for a service provider:

  - Case studies, recent project highlights, before-and-after transformation stories.
  - Your thoughts on changes to your industry/current trends.
  - Frequently-asked-question answers about working with you.
  - Interviews with your current clients that might entice potential clients to engage with your business.

📋 DOUBLE DUTY

- ◆ People like to consume content in different formats. If you write a blog post for your website, send it to your newsletter audience too (or just a snippet that links through to your website's blog). See page 36 for more.

- ◆ You can build your email list (and generate a database of potential clients or customers) by offering something of value as a lead magnet (page 12).

- ◆ If your newsletter is mostly sharing your original written content on a topic, this could provide the backbone for a self-published book (page 96).

☼ ACTION

What is the main strategy behind your newsletter?

☐ Tell people about new products or services

☐ Remind people at regular intervals about my business

☐ Share expertise or insights

☐ _____

☐ _____

☐ _____

How regularly will you send out a newsletter?

☐ Weekly

☐ Monthly

☐ Quarterly

☐ _____

What type of content will your newsletter consist of? Think of 2-3 different types.

_____

_____

_____

_____

List 1-3 topics that could be sent in an automated email sequence after someone has subscribed to your newsletter. The aim of these emails should be to help people know, like and trust you, and prepare them for your regular newsletter.

1 _____

2 _____

3 _____

Research different types of newsletter platforms. Consider the costs and benefits of each:

Platform	Features/perks	Cost per month/year

☐ Set up your newsletter subscription form on your website.

☐ Add your newsletter dates for the next 12 months to your calendar.

☐ Set up your automated email sequence for new newsletter subscribers.

A QUICK CHAT WITH

Jeremy Wortsman

FOUNDER OF THE JACKY WINTER GROUP

I've long admired Jeremy Wortsman, founder of creative representation agency The Jacky Winter Group (JWG), for his ability to invest in ideas and go all-in on self-initiated projects. Over the years, JWG has produced a popular podcast, run a range of live events and exhibitions, and their website is regularly updated with informative and engaging content. In recent years, Jeremy has observed that the artists and illustrators on their platform struggle with having their work seen by diminishing social media audiences. So they developed PencilBooth, a micro-newsletter service built for solo and small businesses to directly reach their clients and followers in the places they are most active.

What's your current vibe re: social media?

I think we're in a great time of experimentation. I am loving seeing people experimenting and working with the energy of the fact that things are really fracturing at the moment. It's an exciting time that allows for new platforms and new mediums to flourish. I think social media isn't going anywhere, but I think it's just getting smaller, and allowing us to tap into niches of people in a new way. It is a painful process though as it's quite taxing on your brain to navigate and requires taking some risks and trying new things out which might not work.

Email newsletters are not a new form of self-promotion. What do you think is the barrier for artists, illustrators, photographers, and other self-employed people to starting their own newsletter on any platform?

As a freelancer you can't put all your eggs in one basket for marketing. Email is still one of the best mediums we have for communicating on the internet and more and more people are craving clarity, simplicity, and a direct relationship with their audience. I can't think of a better platform to do that with. It's like the health food of social media. It takes a bit more effort, and might not taste as good, but it's better for everyone in the long run!

The first issue is that most newsletter platforms are made for writers or for written content. Most artists are doing art because that's the medium they communicate most effectively in, so feeling like you need to become a writer is one barrier. The second one is that email is a very basic platform, and was really only meant for text — doing things like showing rich content, alternative typefaces, etc, is just hard to do. So you have this secondary barrier of the fact that you also need to be a graphic designer to make things look nice. Since email has to cater to so many platforms you have to design for the lowest common denominator — that's a further technical constraint. On top of that, most artists and illustrators just want to be doing their work, not creating capital C 'content', so newsletters just feel like this boring task that is a necessary evil. The biggest challenge is that it's hard to measure engagement. You're not getting likes and comments which really get that dopamine firing, so the immediate rewards are not always apparent.

How does PencilBooth make it easy to start a newsletter?

We put images first and foremost — so you don't get paralysed by a blank canvas. Most people are already prepping heaps of assets for Instagram and other platforms, so PencilBooth can basically just extend the life of that content, and ensure it's getting directly in front of your audience, all in a single template that can't be modified or changed. Limiting sends to once a week max as well builds trust with the audience who know you simply won't be spamming them as well.

What other self-promotion activities have you done to promote Jacky Winter?

A few years ago now, we hosted an event series called Open Tabs. The concept was simple — we approached our clients (who were, at the time, mostly large advertising agencies) and told them if they could give us an audience in a conference room for an hour, we'd bring along four creative people plus drinks and snacks, and each of them would get ten minutes to talk about ten browser tabs they had open.

It remains to this day one of my favourite 'marketing' activities we've ever done at Jacky Winter. We got facetime with some our most valued clients, and it didn't feel like a sales pitch because it wasn't. It was just genuinely a fun hour, and also a chance for me to talk about my favourite topic — random links I found on the internet — while also getting to introduce clients to Jacky Winter artists and other interesting people in our orbit.

PENCILBOOTH.COM
JACKYWINTER.COM

⟨ **14** ⟩

Be social (in real life!)

Given our goal is to get people to like, know and trust us, nothing beats an in-person interaction.

Across my career, there have been a number of instances where choosing to attend an event has been beneficial — 'sliding doors' moments, if you will. At one small gathering that began with a panel discussion and ended with casual drinks, I got chatting with one of the speakers. Soon after, she turned into a client and that relationship turned into thousands of dollars of income, other client referrals, and a supportive peer relationship, too. At that same event, I met a copywriter who had just launched a podcast. After the event, she invited me to be a guest on her show (and I hired her for some copywriting projects, too!). My own experience meeting and engaging with people through events I have attended has resulted in product sales, speaking engagements, and many other community-building benefits.

The COVID years dampened the incentives to get out and meet people, be it at networking groups, conferences, social events and the like — while at the same time, online meeting platforms grew in number and popularity. But meeting people face-to-face will always be more memorable and impactful than digital interactions.

Whether it's a large conference or summit, a workshop or talk, or a one-on-one coffee catchup, the return on investment for connections with clients, customers and peers can be well worth the effort.

TIPS AND IDEAS

◆ If you find interacting socially within large events difficult or depleting, try these tips:

- Attend events with a friend or colleague.
- Set small goals for yourself, such as talking to one new person.
- Arrive early to events, when they are less crowded and overwhelming.

- Have an exit strategy in place, but allow yourself time to settle in before you deploy it!
- Practice your elevator pitch or a few conversation starters before the event.
- Focus on listening and asking questions, rather than feeling pressure to talk about yourself.
- Remember that most people are also nervous in social situations.
- Host your own event! See page 45 for more about that.

♦ Conferences often have opportunities to connect and network with others built into the program. This can be in the form of workshops, demonstrations, dinners, or drinks. But you can also start small by simply connecting with the people sitting around you.

♦ Events held by professional associations and membership groups are an easy way to build a community of peers, find mentors, or potential clients.

♦ Getting involved in local community events helps to make connections with peers inside and around your industry. Websites such as Eventbrite, Meetup, WeTeachMe and ClassBento list events by location and interest.

♦ Classes or workshops can be a more intimate way to meet other likeminded people, especially if they are held regularly.

♦ If it is a small event, make an effort to connect with the event host prior (perhaps via email or social media). When you arrive, seek out that person — hosts are often more than happy to chat with attendees and help to introduce them to others.

♦ If you think the event was successful, rewarding or fun, tell the host. It takes a lot of effort, and who doesn't love a genuine compliment?

♦ When attending an event, come prepared. If you introduce yourself or are introduced to someone, be able to succinctly explain your business or service offering. See page 22 for tips.

♦ Establishing connections also means being a connector. Recommending a person or business to someone else will establish you as the link, and can increase your social capital. So, make introductions where you see a benefit or alignment of minds and services.

♦ Travelling? Consider adding a professional event or in-person meetup to your itinerary. Not only will it expand your potential network outside of your usual setting, you can gather insights from locals you might not otherwise have gathered as a visitor.

☐ NOT APPLICABLE   ☐ SOMETHING TO CONSIDER   ☐ YES, DO IT!

- ◆ Professional organisations often host a range of events for its members to meet, network, and develop their professional skillset.

- ◆ Ways to follow up with people that you meet at real-life events include exchanging contact details (printed marketing materials are put to good use here — see page 64), sending an email, or subscribing to their newsletter.

- ◆ When reaching out to a professional connection and asking if they would be willing to meet for coffee, be clear about your intentions and explain why you think connecting with them would be beneficial for both parties. Keep the message concise and respectful, but don't be discouraged if the answer is no.

☼ ACTION

☐ Search event websites or member organisations that host local events.

☐ Subscribe to the mailing lists of organisations that regularly hold networking/ social events, talks, or workshops.

☐ Contact a friend or colleague to be your +1.

List 3 or more events you could attend in the next 3-6 months.

1 _____

2 _____

3 _____

_____

_____

List 3 or more people you want to connect (or reconnect) with in person:

_____

_____

_____

_____

_____

Host an event

I have organised, hosted, and assisted at events for the creative community at various points across my career. Talks, panel discussions, meet-ups, markets, dinners, lunches. There was always an air of informality about them as my main motivation was to build and maintain a community of peers in a city that I was relatively new to.

Initially I tapped into an existing group that regularly organised informal gatherings amongst creative professionals, but I soon found myself volunteering to take the wheel. Despite my natural tendencies as an introvert, being at the helm of a community group and organising events gave me courage, and my social nervousness dissipated. There was always something to do, and it felt natural to talk to and connect with people who attended the events. I also relished the opportunity to approach people I admired and ask them to speak at the events.

Visibility is strong when you take the lead or are the go-to person at an event.

 TIPS AND IDEAS

◆ Organise a panel of speakers to address common issues or roadblocks your customers face.

◆ Invite loyal customers or clients, or those who spend over a certain amount each year, to a special event where they can get to know you better, or engage with your business in a different way. This strategy also helps build word-of-mouth and brand loyalty.

◆ Don't forget about your suppliers and collaborators — events that connect these people with each other.

◆ Bringing in sponsors or collaborators for an event can not only help distribute running costs, but can be a way to cross-promote your event to new audiences.

SELF-PROMOTION WITHOUT SOCIAL MEDIA

◆ Meetups or events for people within your industry (your peers) can be helpful for finding collaborators, mentors, and colleagues to share work between.

◆ Even if you don't have a large network or audience to promote your event to yet, there are ways to drive attendance. List your workshops on local event listing websites or ticketing marketplaces, or host one as part of a community festival.

◆ Online events can reach a broader audience that would otherwise find a local event a barrier. It is slightly more difficult to connect one-on-one with attendees, but with options like break-out rooms and chat groups, more personal connections can be fostered.

◆ Event ideas:
- Open studio
- Demonstration
- Art exhibition
- Launch
- VIP client/customer thank you drinks
- Panel events
- Guest speaker talk

◆ If you don't want to organise and host your own event, but you have a workspace that is ideal for that kind of activity, offer your work space to people who organise events that attract your ideal customers and clients.

DOUBLE DUTY

◆ Hosting an event is an opportunity to distribute your printed marketing collateral (page 64), or build a mailing list (page 36).

◆ You can collaborate with sponsors who might distribute the event information to their networks (page 78).

◆ Talks and panels can be recorded as a podcast (page 85) or video content (page 54). Just make sure you get a release from the participant/s.

◆ You can host an event as part of a philanthropic activity (page 48), or help to run an event as a volunteer (page 51).

◆ Collaborative projects or self-initiated projects can benefit from having an in-person event as a promotional activity. See page 104 for more.

☀ ACTION

Type of event:

☐ Panel   ☐ Launch   ☐ _____

☐ Talk   ☐ Casual/social event   ☐ _____

Potential date/s:

_____

_____

Location/s:

_____

_____

Budget

Venue: _____

Refreshments: _____

Audio visual/tech: _____

Other: _____

_____

_____

_____

Marketing collateral required:

_____

_____

Who's on your team?

Before event: _____

During event: _____

⚙ **16**

Be philanthropic

Philanthropy, such as making donations of money, goods or services to charities or not-for-profits (NFPs), can be a way to find values-aligned customers and clients, and develop trust and likeability with your audience. It can also give you exposure to an audience who might otherwise not know about or engage with your services or products.

Of course, there are potential downsides to using philanthropy as a self-promotion tool. One is the perception of 'virtue signaling,' in which a business is seen as using charitable donations solely for the purpose of promoting itself rather than genuinely caring about the cause. It's important to ensure that any philanthropic efforts are authentic and aligned with the values and mission of the business, rather than just a marketing tactic. Additionally, it's important to carefully evaluate the impact of any donations to ensure that they are actually making a positive difference rather than just being a PR move.

⟡ TIPS AND IDEAS

- ◆ Donate a percentage of profits to a charity or cause, either for a specific time period or as a consistent percentage of your overall revenue.

- ◆ Donating products or services directly to a charity or cause, such as prizes in a silent auction.

- ◆ Sponsor a charity event or program. If you can be the only business in your 'category' to sponsor an event that has a lot of sponsors, it can have impact.

- ◆ Host a fundraising event or campaign to benefit a charity or cause.

- ◆ If you run an educational course or workshop, a scholarship can be a way to offer it to a student who might otherwise not have the means to participate.

- ◆ Partner with a charity or cause to create a co-branded product.

◆ Offer your services at a reduced rate or without charge (pro-bono) to a charity or cause. Some businesses dedicate time and effort to pro-bono services for a specific number of clients or type of client per year.

◆ If philanthropy is built into your business' marketing and promotion efforts, make sure you follow through on the donation in a timely manner. It might seem obvious, but we have all heard stories of businesses who talk up their charity giving but fail to deliver on their promises. In a world where consumers want to 'see the receipts', make sure you can realistically deliver on the promise before making it a part of your self-promotion plan.

DOUBLE DUTY

◆ The benefits of volunteering, donating, or working with a charity or non-profit organisation to support their goals go beyond self-promotion! Your efforts or funds will support the work they do, and you'll get a dose of good feelings, too.

◆ Investigate the opportunity to meet and connect with others who are also involved in the charity for philanthropic reasons, such as those who are involved in investment or on the board of directors.

ACTION

List out some charitable *causes* that you strongly support. Avoid naming specific charities at this stage.

_____

_____

_____

_____

_____

_____

_____

Narrow your list down to 2-3, thinking about whether your ideal customer or client might also align with these causes.

_____

_____

_____

_____

Research charities both large and small who work to support these causes. Remember that sometimes it is the smaller charities who need the most help.

_____

_____

_____

_____

Contact the charity/NFP to ascertain if there is a need for your product/service, or another way you can assist.

_____

_____

_____

_____

With this information at hand, brainstorm how to combine a charitable donation or effort with your overall self-promotion plan.

_____

_____

_____

_____

_____

_____

17

THE POWER OF VOLUNTEERING

I have volunteered for different organisations and in different capacities over my career—from leading a non-profit association, to joining a community organisation committee, to providing professional services pro-bono, or showing up for a few hours to do a specific duty. Whether it was a regular commitment or a one-off, it meant a lot to me and I have always come away from the experience with valuable insights that I can apply to my business—and in most cases, new connections with likeminded people.

Depending on the nature of the role, volunteering offers a platform to meet and interact with people who could become clients, customers, or collaborators. It also provides an opportunity to showcase your skills, work ethics, and passion for a particular field. Volunteering can also be a source of content that helps potential customers and clients to know, like and trust you—but like philanthropy, the focus should always benefit the charity or organisation you're supporting with your time and efforts.

A QUICK CHAT WITH

Yvonne Meng

CO-FOUNDER OF CIRCLE STUDIO ARCHITECTS

Yvonne is the kind of person whose skills and interests continue to unfurl the longer you know her. Outside of running her boutique architecture firm, she is a talented painter, writer, and circus gymnast (!). I've always admired (and been grateful for) the time, attention, and skill she lends to volunteering for industry associations, which is how we originally met.

What's your current vibe re: social media?

I am *terrible* with social media for both myself and my business. My dogs' account on the other hand is going gangbusters and I post a lot more for them than I do for my business!

I do enjoy Instagram in small doses, but I try to stop myself from scrolling too much as sometimes I find it hard not to compare myself with everyone's curated version of themselves. I use Instagram mostly to scope out businesses, artists, and organisations, rather than actively creating content. I know I should do this more, but in the scheme of all the other things that need doing in a small business, it often falls to the bottom of the pile. Also, in architecture it takes a long time (often years) to finish a project. I always feel like we don't have enough completed work to consistently feed the Instagram machine. I tend to post a lot when something has been completed, but not at other times.

What is the most effective form of marketing for your firm?

Most of our clients come from word of mouth — for example, through past clients or builders. We submit our projects to websites and publications once they're photo-graphed and that has been helpful in getting our work seen by potential clients. I definitely notice an uptick of enquiries after something has been published.

Why do you think investing time in volunteering for industry associations and business groups is good for self-promotion and relationship building?

I have always felt uncomfortable 'marketing' myself. Perhaps some of it is a cultural thing—my parents are Chinese, and whilst I was raised and schooled in Australia, my parents instilled modesty over self-promotion, which was regarded negatively as bragging. I've always loved being a part of a community though, and volunteering in industry bodies and groups has helped me feel connected with others.

Being involved in associations and communities means that I am not explicitly 'self-promoting', rather I'm building relationships which is a lot more meaningful for me. Having a shared goal to focus on (such as putting on an event, or writing for a publication) takes the pressure off needing to promote myself, or 'convert' (I hate that term!) connections into clients. You can just enjoy being involved meeting new people, and if something comes out of it, that's a bonus.

I've attended a few business networking events early on [in my business], which involved people being awkward or aggressively handing out business cards. I don't remember a single person from any of those situations. But I do remember the people I volunteered with over a period of weeks, months, or years and I'm much more likely to recommend them to other people or engage them myself.

Have you done any self-initiated or pro-bono/reduced rate projects as a part of your firm? What were some of the challenges, highlights, and/or unexpected benefits of these projects?

We have done a couple of reduced-fee projects for not-for-profit organisations. Some of these types of projects would be very difficult to get off the ground if they were charged commercial rates. We are essentially donating some of our time to a cause that we believe in and for us to take on a reduced-fee project, our values need to align. The challenge of these projects is that as a small business, it can be hard to manage time and resources. It can be good for exposure depending on the business so each case needs to be weighed up.

I am a strong believer of not working for free so with that perspective, I am not interested in entering design 'competitions' where architects are invited to submit proposals, as they can be quite exploitative. Designers create a lot of intellectual property but often don't get remunerated properly, if at all. Even though it can provide exposure to lesser known firms, I don't agree with the competition system.

CIRCLE.STUDIO

SELF-PROMOTION WITHOUT SOCIAL MEDIA

{18}

Create evergreen video content

Over the years, social media platform algorithms have started to favour video content over still photos. While off-the-cuff video content can work as a self-promotion activity, especially if it feels personal and offers insight into your personality or process, being in front of the camera is not for everyone.

One way to capitalise on the power of search engines is to create informative and educational videos in service of your business, and host them on platforms like YouTube. It's the second-largest search engine in the world, with over 2 billion monthly active users.

Certain types of video content, such as 'how-to' videos, can be a great resource for people using search engines to answer their questions. These videos can be pre-planned, produced to a high quality, and offer potential customers and clients just enough insight into your personality and process to establish a strong connection with your business.

Even if creating video content is not a part of your primary marketing strategy, there is still value to be gained from creating 'evergreen' video content.

 TIPS AND IDEAS

- Create a content plan for your video or series, for example:
    - address frequently asked questions from a potential client or customer regarding your services
    - show off the features, outcomes or benefits of your products or services
    - demonstrate how your customer can use/display your product; and/or
    - demonstrate how your customer can care for their product.
- Think about where you could shoot the video/s. The space needs to be quiet and with adequate lighting.

- Approach the content of a video like a how-to blog post or brand-building newsletter. Address pain points your potential customer could be experiencing that your service or product could help with. It might show an example of the product in use, or a case study from a previous customer or client.

- Remember to shoot your video in landscape format for best viewing on platforms like YouTube and your website.

- Don't rely on selfie-style camera holding. Grab a friend, or a tripod. Test different lighting options, and make sure your audio recording is not muffled, echoey, or interrupted with background noise.

- If your video will have multiple scenes, use a story board to plot them out so that you know everything you need to shoot before you begin.

- Use an autocue app if you need help remembering your lines.

- If your video features people other than just yourself, ask them to sign a release (an agreement that grants you permission to use their recorded likeness).

- Add video captioning and a transcript to make your video more accessible.

- Include links in your video caption so that viewers can find your website and learn more about your products or services.

- Don't forget to apply your visual branding elements to the video and to your video platform account.

DOUBLE DUTY

- A video uploaded to a platform like YouTube or Vimeo can be embedded on your website (page 8).

- Multiple videos can form the basis of a course that can be offered for sale or as a lead magnet for newsletter subscribers (page 12).

- If you have a podcast, you can video record it live, or simply upload the audio (and a static visual) to YouTube, capitalising on the platform's search engine capabilities (page 85).

☀ ACTION

List at least 3 topics (but more if you can!) that you could record a video about to help educate potential clients or customers.

_____

_____

_____

_____

_____

_____

_____

_____

Location requirements:

_____

_____

_____

Tech requirements (video, audio, editing, music, graphics etc):

_____

_____

_____

Who's on your team?

_____

_____

_____

_____

⚡

It's okay to unfollow, mute or snooze
people you follow on social media who
give you that little twinge of jealousy,
anxiety, or self-doubt. Be conscious of
when those feelings arise, and take action.

✦ 19 ✦

Keep your branding consistent

Think of the worst date you ever went on: the person sitting across from you looked nothing like you expected, or they treated you differently in person to how they spoke online. The vibe was just off.

That's how you turn off a potential customer or client: using a visual language and tone of voice in one space that is different to how your business appears in another space. It's confusing. Visitors to your website might not have come from a search engine result, but from an inbound link such as product packaging, a cross-promoted blog post or a customer's share on social media.

Customers will make a series of split-second decisions about your business when they see it displayed in any format — from packaging to a physical store, a social media feed to an email. It's important that these visitors — who may have already experienced your business' visual branding in another context — don't have a jarring or confusing first impression. Your logo, colour palette, typefaces, and photographic or illustrative image style should all help visitors connect your website to other promotional platforms that feature your business.

You also don't want to feel *embarrassed* by your business' look and feel. This is something I encounter frequently in my line of work: clients approach me because they don't feel confident handing out a business card or sending people to their website when it feels misaligned with how they want to present themselves to the world.

As a designer, I'm obviously fairly passionate (read: biased!) about this topic. But I also believe that when you're running a business you're making dozens of decisions every day. Decision fatigue is a real thing, and can lead to procrastination about larger marketing decisions. Being consistent with your branding can reduce the need to make regular decisions about how to present your business in your self-promotion.

TIPS AND IDEAS

◆ Assess your other online spaces for branding consistency. If you promote your website via Instagram, does your feed visually mirror your website through the use of colours, logo, imagery, or overall vibe? What about your printed marketing material, packaging, or email newsletter? Make visual updates as necessary so that each space has a similar feel to the others.

Colours, fonts and logos:

◆ The foundations of a strong visual brand are the consistent use of colour, fonts, branding elements like a logo, and imagery. This visual language should distinguish you from peers and competitors — make sure your branding colour palette or fonts aren't going to be confused with another business in your industry.

◆ It's best not to use too many different fonts, although a variety of versions of a single font family (Helvetica regular, Helvetica italic and Helvetica bold etc) makes sense and helps you add visual interest to a design without it feeling chaotic.

◆ If you're just starting out, begin by using 1–2 fonts (or font families) and 1–2 colours consistently, with your logo if you have one, and make sure all of your marketing elements reflect this combination of visual branding.

◆ Almost all fonts come with a licence. Sometimes, free fonts say they are for 'personal use only' — which means you shouldn't use them as part of your visual branding and you definitely shouldn't use them for your logo. Respect the creators of these incredibly complex pieces of software and pay for a licensed font where you can — most average about $30.

◆ Make yourself a mini cheat sheet where you write down your colour codes and the fonts you want to use consistently so you stay on track and start out strong, because it is very easy to get excited and start using all the fonts and all the colours. Having a Style Guide will help to reduce decision-making with how your business is presented across marketing collateral, and will keep things looking consistent. See page 62 for a mini style guide template.

◆ Providing sufficient contrast between the text colour and background colour make content available to a wider range of people, including those with visual impairments, eye strain or fatigue.

Photos and imagery:

- Your image style is part of your visual identity. Consistently average or low-quality imagery probably won't show off the quality of your work in the way you intend it to be experienced. High quality imagery is really worth investing in if you want to communicate yourself in a professional way. It drives aspiration and can increase the perceived value of your product.

- Be strategic about what you're photographing if you're investing in a professional photographer and/or stylist. And make sure that this type of high-quality content is reusable and perhaps can be repurposed to make the most of your investment.

Tone of voice:

- The 'tone of voice' here is how you write or speak to your audience, and should also be consistent. Your tone should be carefully crafted to reflect your business' values, culture, and goals. A friendly and conversational tone is suitable for a business that wants to establish a personal connection with its audience. A professional and formal tone might be more appropriate for a business that wants to convey competence and expertise. There can definitely be a combination of friendly and professional, as long as it feels authentic for your audience and the tone is consistent.

- A copywriter can help set the tone for your business' communication. They can provide guides for email, newsletters, and other written communication that can be very helpful when you have staff or subcontractors and want to maintain a consistent tone of voice.

Established businesses:

- If you've been in business for a while, and you think your branding has gone off track a bit over the years, stand back and take a critical look. Tweak or simplify — bring it back to what still feels right. Ask outsiders for their opinion — sometimes, it's actually all in our heads and we just think we're not being consistent because we're too close to it, or, we're bored and think we need to change.

- Gather an example of everything that features your visual identity: what stands out as being 'not like the others'? What can be consolidated? What still looks great and feels true to the branding, and what needs an update?

When to call in a professional:

- Investing in a professional graphic designer, photographer, or copywriter is definitely the way to go when you want your visual branding and tone of voice to look and feel cohesive. These service providers are trained in the technical tools, giving your business high quality brand assets, ready-to-go templates and brand guides — so you can concentrate on what you do best. But as individuals, they are also often called to their profession because of an innate skillset mixed with a strategic business acumen focused on communication and messaging. They can offer insights and perspective that you can't see when you are too close to your business. Use these satellite team members to strengthen your self-promotion arsenal.

▯▯ DOUBLE DUTY

◆ A strong visual identity can inform the design of your website (page 8), printed collateral (page 64) and packaging (page 71).

☀ ACTION

Collect an example of every piece of collateral that promotes your business — both printed and digital. What stands out? What do you love? What needs modifying, changing, or tweaking?

_____

_____

_____

_____

_____

Research and list service providers (e.g. designers, photographers, copywriters) whose work you think aligns with the vision you have for your business' branding:

_____

_____

_____

_____

_____

☐ Make a list of collateral you want to create or update.

MINI STYLE GUIDE TEMPLATE

Colours

Attach colour sample	Attach colour sample	Attach colour sample
#	#	#
R G B	R G B	R G B
C M Y K	C M Y K	C M Y K

Typography

	Font	Size	Colour
Headings			
Subhead 1			
Subhead 2			
Body text			

Tone of voice

Describe your tone of voice in 3 adjectives:

1 _____

2 _____

3 _____

We don't say:	We say:
e.g. 'hey guys'	e.g. 'hey folks / team / friends'

P.S. YOU CAN DOWNLOAD A PRINTABLE COPY OF THIS CHEAT SHEET AT CREATIVEMINDSHQ.COM

20

THE POWER OF PINTEREST

Pinterest might have some of the qualities of a social media site (lovely visuals, like and sharing buttons, a slightly addictive quality), but in reality, it is a search engine and bookmarking tool. And when you use it strategically, it can be an excellent platform for self-promotion.

Pinterest users favour content that is visually appealing and high-quality, so you can repurpose your social media content, and use keywords in your descriptions to make your content more searchable. The platform also has lots of resources to help you optimise your content.

Start by identifying a goal for your Pinterest self-promotion, such as building your email list or sending traffic to particular products in your online shop. Focusing on a small goal will make analysing the traffic Pinterest brings to your website or mailing list easier to see if it is working for you.

Creating a business account on Pinterest can give you access to more tools and engagement analytics, so you can build on any traction you gain.

21

Invest in printed marketing collateral

Despite the ubiquity of digital devices and content in our lives, humans are still captivated by print.

On a recent outing, I came across an event space in a neighbourhood near where I live. It was large and well-appointed, with a variety of rooms for hire. At the time, I was investigating options for hosting an event (to support the release of this very book, in fact!). I enquired at the front desk if they had a brochure or price list that I could take with me. They did not—instead directing me to scan a QR code and find out more from their website.

I took a cursory look at the website as I left the premises. In fairness, their website was well designed. Most of the info I needed was there. But it soon became lost in my phone's digital mess of closed tabs and assorted distractions. I promptly forgot about it (I can't actually remember the name of the place now). Had a brochure, business card, or other tangible item with basic information about their offering left with me that day it likely would have travelled with my other important possessions in my bag, to my home, stuck to the fridge or the pinboard near my desk—an unobtrusive but constant reminder of its presence in the world and the solution to a need I had.

Printed items and their tangible quality create memories in a different way to digital interactions. While they can be thrown out, they can also be kept, reused, and remind customers and clients of your business in a way that isn't ephemeral.

 TIPS AND IDEAS

- The design and quality of your printed items will likely inform how disposable they are—consider how your printed marketing collateral can become more like a keepsake for your customer or client.

- Providing items like business cards or flyers can offer prospective customers or clients a physical reminder of your brand to hold onto.

- The quality of the materials you print with can evoke feelings about your business that aren't as easy to portray digitally — such as luxurious, creative, or environmentally conscious.

- If your business services a local area, letterbox flyers can target a hyper-local customer base.

- Fridge magnets can mean your business is at the heart of the household.

- Print marketing, like books, still evokes a special type of trust in customers that digital marketing doesn't.

- While you might think flashy animated graphics and sound will grab attention, it's often the case that simple and 'quiet' printed items are more effective at holding it. They require a type of focus that makes them more memorable.

- If you are reluctant to invest in printed paper materials to promote your business for environmental reasons — i.e. you see them as wasting paper or ending up as waste — specify a higher quality (yet responsible or recyclable) paper or card and vegetable-based inks.

DOUBLE DUTY

- Printed items work well when you are encountering customers or clients in person, such as at networking events, trade shows, markets, workshops or demonstrations (pages 42, 45, 74 and 93).

- You could create printed items specifically for your retailers (page 32).

- Printed items can be added to product packaging (page 71).

- Printed items can double as merchandise (page 101).

☀ ACTION

☐ Collect or photograph samples of printed marketing material that appeal to you — be it packaging, business cards, flyers, magnets, wrapping paper, bookmarks.

Here are some suggestions for brand-aligned printed collateral that a business can produce to market and advertise its products and services. Circle ideas that resonate with your business:

☐ Brochures

☐ Flyers

☐ Business cards

☐ Postcards

☐ Banners

☐ Posters

☐ Catalogues or product info cards

☐ Care cards

☐ Thank you cards

☐ Size and product info labels

☐ Bookmarks

☐ Maps/location guides

☐ Price list

☐ Bill posters

☐ Wrapping paper

☐ Ribbon

☐ Pins and badges

☐ Coasters

☐ Recipe cards

☐ Magnets

☐ Coupons

☐ Stickers

☐ Envelopes

Research designers and printers who can create marketing collateral for your business:

_____

_____

_____

_____

_____

_____

_____

_____

—⚡—

When deciding where to focus your
self-promotion energy, ask yourself:

- Does this increase my visibility to my
  ideal audience? (And is that audience
  new, existing or aligned?)

- Can this 'content' be repurposed,
  reshared on multiple platforms or
  networks; does it have a long lifespan?

- Will I learn anything, or flex a muscle
  that I can use to create or increase
  revenue in my business?

- Even if I can't predict the ultimate
  outcome, will I enjoy the process?

A QUICK CHAT WITH

Jenna Hipgrave

CO-FOUNDER OF THE HUNGRY WORKSHOP

Jenna and I met years ago when offered to create a custom bookmark for my first book, *Conversations with Creative Women*. Jenna and her partner, Simon, had just moved to Melbourne to establish their letterpress and design business. I, of course, jumped at the chance to showcase their beautiful work to my readers, and a friendship, built on a love of all things print and design, was formed. Today, The Hungry Workshop is an award-winning letterpress print and design studio that employs a small team, and they regularly use their skills and self-initiated studio projects to raise funds for under-resourced communities and causes.

What's your current vibe re: social media?

We were somewhat lucky with social media back in the day. We launched Hungry Workshop when Instagram was just starting to gain traction. We love sharing insights into our process, projects and tools. However, the platform has shifted in the 12 years we've been using it. The algorithm has transformed the platform into a bit of a beast that must be fed, regularly.

We've shifted from posting organically into a more strategic approach that is constantly shifting its appetite. One moment the advice is we must do videos, then its reels, now still images are back! It's hard to keep up with and sometimes I simply don't have the energy to feed it. We've dabbled in the other platforms, but it's hard to create engaging and authentic content for a platform you don't regularly consume yourself.

Why do you think investing in well-designed printed collateral and packaging is good for self-promotion and relationship building?

We've all had the joy of finding a box of old photos, a box of childhood notes, our grandmother's favourite recipe scribbled on the back of a receipt, a postcard from a loved one overseas. In that moment, we're transported back and connected with our past selves, that person who tucked away that precious piece of paper.

In a world where everything changes, print is real, it's concrete, it's tangible. With printed collateral and packaging you create connections, you create a moment, you give people something physical to remember you by.

A business card becomes a memento, a reminder of your connection, a card that can hold the promise and hope for the future.

Packaging is an extension of your brand, a way to communicate how much you care about your product, an opportunity to create a moment of anticipation or a moment of joy.

A thank you note becomes a connection between the maker and creator and you. A note to say thank you. A note to say we appreciate your support.

Print is grounding. Tactility brings us back into the moment. It reminds us that we're here, in the now. It's a moment that's all yours, free from distraction and interruption. It's intimate and personal to be in someone's physical space, and that moment should be suitably respected. If you're going to be there, do it with intention and put your best foot forward.

Tell us about some of the philanthropic projects you have coordinated as a part of your business (challenges, highlights, outcomes, unexpected benefits, etc)

Many years ago, when our business was very young and Brisbane was flooding, we pulled together a fundraising exhibition called Queenslake. We didn't have the skills to help people rebuild their homes, but we could offer our support in the way of fundraising.

Our first exhibition gave us the confidence to ask for help. We contacted all sorts of designers and illustrators — people whose work we loved, and many of them said yes, they would love to contribute. We connected with our design community, gave everyone a chance to help and unexpectedly promoted Hungry Workshop to a larger network.

The last exhibition we held was in December 2019, right before our world changed. The exhibition was titled Twenty Six, a collaboration with Pop & Pac and Bone Digital. We asked 26 designers to create a letter of the alphabet and letterpress printed a set of limited-edition prints. The network of people at the event made it a big success — we raised over $14,000 for The Australian Literacy and Numeracy Foundation!

Exhibitions have become a part of our story. They are a way we can give back to our community, through creating an event that connects people, celebrating the work of our fellow creatives and supporting charities through fundraising. The artwork then lives on in people's homes and studios. The stories of the artwork and the exhibition become part of the story people tell.

Tell us about some memorable clients that have come from relationship building or self-promotion activities that weren't just 'social media content'.

We often do the kind of work we want to do before people ask us to create it for them.

During the COVID lockdowns, as our work was interrupted and our lives were turned upside down, we created a stationery brand called Off–Line. The idea was to create a notebook that gives back more than it takes, along with celebrating and supporting the environment and mental health.

The notebooks are very subtly branded, with the Off–Line logo only appearing in the inside back cover and Hungry Workshop simply mentioned in a line of type. We didn't intend for the Off–Line notebooks to be self-promotion, but surprisingly they have been fantastic tools for extending our brand and creating new opportunities. We have since created sets of custom notebooks for a variety of brands to share with their communities and networks. A notebook isn't simply used once and recycled, it lives in your bag or on your desk, you hold it in your hands, it gets tattered and used, filled with your notes, ideas and sketches.

We lead by example, by doing the work we want to do and sharing it with our friends and peers. We often find that this is the best path to finding new opportunities to do the work we love doing.

HUNGRYWORKSHOP.COM.AU

22

Invest in your packaging

If you run a product-based business, your packaging design can be a highly effective way to promote your business and create a positive experience for your customers.

As I look around my home, I can identify several packaging items that have found a permanent function amongst my belongings. Storage containers, boxes large and small, cloth bags — when produced to a high quality, they can become regular reminders of your brand when retained by your customer.

Not only can packaging help to sell your product by catching the eye of customers scanning a shelf, or delight them as they open a delivery, your packaging design can also communicate important information about your brand, such as your values and mission. Well-designed packaging can help build brand recognition and loyalty, which can lead to increased customer engagement and a higher likelihood of repeat purchases.

 TIPS AND IDEAS

- You don't necessarily need to break the bank to create effective packaging. If you are on a budget, consider customising pre-fabricated packaging. Economic additions such as stickers, tape, or stamps are small details that can make a big impact on the overall look and feel of your packaging.

- You might be able to have a one-size-fits-all purchases approach to packaging, or develop a few sizes that will cover the majority of all purchase combinations.

- Closed-loop packaging refers to a system in which packaging materials are recycled or reused to create new packaging. This approach aims to reduce waste and minimize the environmental impact of packaging. For example, you might offer customers the option to return used packaging for recycling or reuse for another customer's order.

- You could include a product catalogue, brochure, or QR code that leads to a landing page featuring other products or special deals.

- A packaging option that is kept and reused by customers might actually be helping you in the long-term, as it continues to remind the customer of your business.

- Packaging should reflect the value of the product, but also the values of your business. If environmental sustainability is important to your business' values, scrutinise how your packaging materials reflect this value.

- Consider adding a personal touch to the packaging, such as a handwritten note or a personalised sticker with the customer's name.

- Make sure that all packaging elements are consistent and align with your overall brand strategy. If a customer has purchased a product from your online store and the packaging arrives with a different brand logo or colour palette, it sends a mixed message about your brand.

- Designing packaging for social media 'shareability' in mind can help you reach a social media audience through your *customer's* networks.

- Consider how your product packaging will protect your customer's purchase in transit. When experimenting with different packaging options, send yourself (or a friend) a test via various postage methods. Note how the package arrives and the experience of it from a visual branding perspective.

- Sadly, package thievery is a by-product of a society that shops online and has packages delivered to our front doors. If your packaging looks irresistible, consider how this might be seen from the street. Then, suggest instructions to your customer about where and how they would like to receive their delivery.

⊟⊟ DOUBLE DUTY

- Your packaging could catch the attention of customers in a retail setting, which is something retailers love (page 32).

- Use the 'unboxing' experience to encourage recipients to leave a positive review for your business (page 4) or to share it to their social media audience.

ACTION

Determine your budget for packaging design/redesign and materials. This should be reflective of the value of the product you are sending the customer — after all, you will likely need to absorb this cost into your product cost or add it to a packing and delivery fee.

Packaging cost per sale (ballpark):

_____

_____

_____

_____

What are the different sizes of the products? Jot down dimensions here:

1 _____

2 _____

3 _____

Are there any prefabricated options that you could use for some or all of your packaging needs? List them here:

_____

_____

_____

_____

_____

_____

_____

_____

23

Exhibit at trade shows, markets and fairs

Markets, fairs and trade shows, or any short term exhibition of your work, can be great places for relationship and community building.

Years ago, I had a side-project making and selling handmade jewellery and access-ories. I was still running my graphic design business, but through this side project I exhibited at local design markets and was featured on various directories and blogs. At one market, held inside a beautiful historic building near Melbourne's city centre, my stall was positioned next to a maker who also had a main service-based business as a copywriter. As we chatted between customers, we became fast friends and, eventually, clients of each other's service-based businesses. She remains one of my closest friends today, and it was not lost on us the power of that one market day when, years later, I attended her wedding in that very same building.

Whether you're there as a trader or a customer, trade shows and markets can be a highly effective way to promote your brand and increase your visibility in your industry. Depending on your strategy, it's a proven way to develop retail relationships, build a community of supportive peers, and develop your customer experience beyond the screen of online commerce.

 TIPS AND IDEAS

- Offer promotions or discounts at the event so that you have an opportunity to engage with people in a personable, more meaningful way.

- Research the event beforehand to ensure it is a good fit for your brand and target audience.

- Invest in a well-designed booth that creates a welcoming atmosphere to attract customers.

- Introduce yourself to the organisers or hosts.

- Experiment with the design of your stall and consider how it can be eye-catching through the use of height, signage, lighting and product display.

- Attend events organised by the market or trade show that are designed to allow stallholders and retail customers to meet and mingle.

- Ensure you've read any stallholder materials provided by the event organisers, especially where it relates to inclusions or restrictions on your display.

- Do a recce (a reconnaissance mission) before committing to a stall. Attend trade shows and markets that you think you could exhibit at, and observe:

  - The kind of customer in attendance
  - Which stalls appear to get the most customers, or that visitors make a beeline to
  - The kind of promotional material stallholders have on display
  - The kind of packaging customers receive
  - Satellite events designed to help traders meet and connect with customers in a non-transactional way such as workshops or demonstrations.

- Trade shows and markets are often held over one or many days. When you include set up and pack down, the time required for you to be present at your stall can add up. Consider who is on hand to help with preparation, setup, helping customers and covering you for breaks so your energy stores can be used to build connections.

- Checklists will be your friend when you are preparing yourself as a trader.

- Demonstrate how products can be used in practice or display them in situ.

- Meet other vendors and industry professionals at the event.

- Follow up with leads after the event to build relationships and future collaborations.

▣ DOUBLE DUTY

- These types of trader events can be a place to offer a demonstration or workshop (page 93), and/or nurture retailer relationships (page 32).

- Some trade shows and markets offer stallholders a listing on a public online directory or in marketing material (page 18).

- Many markets and trade shows now offer education and networking events for stall holders and industry peers to meet in person (page 42).

☐ NOT APPLICABLE   ☐ SOMETHING TO CONSIDER   ☐ YES, DO IT!

ACTION

Research trade shows, fairs or markets that target your ideal customer. List your findings below.

Market name	Fee	Frequency	Location	Duration

List what you already have in place to participate in a market, fair or trade show:

_____

_____

_____

_____

_____

_____

List what you need to do to increase your stock for a trade show or market:

_____

_____

_____

_____

_____

_____

_____

Rough out a budget for investing in a trade show or market. Don't forget about costs associated with being present (or having staff represent your business for you) including transport, refreshments, overtime, childcare, etc.

_____

_____

_____

List your goals for doing the market or trade show. What would success or a sound return on the investment look like?

_____

_____

_____

_____

Visualise and sketch your market stall setup!

✻ **24** ✻

Collaborate

Collaborations from a marketing perspective are powerful in that they hope to introduce two audiences who are aligned but perhaps not (yet) overlapping.

You can also use collaborations for social causes that you're passionate about, and to do something outside of your normal practice. A collaboration can also generate excitement with audiences as two brands combine their best service or product into one amazing offer.

If you choose collaborations strategically, they can boost both your product output and your marketing output because you're pooling resources, you're creating content together, and you're building each other's audiences.

 TIPS AND IDEAS

- The concept of 'collaboration' can have lots of meanings to different people in business. What it shouldn't mean by default is 'business X creates something for use by business Y in exchange for "exposure".'

- Collaborations come in all shapes and sizes. Whether it be a co-production, a co-hosting opportunity, or a licensing arrangement, there needs to be a fair exchange of value—tangible or not—for both parties.

- If you have an idea for a collaboration but you don't know the other party personally, be strategic about how you ask the collaborator. You should do your research and be able to justify the outcomes for both parties. A pitch with some lovely graphics could sweeten the offer.

- Ensure you have a contract or agreement in place to set clear expectations and responsibilities of both parties for the life of the collaboration. Who is paying for what? How is each party credited? Who does what?

- A collaboration might come in the form of licensing an element of a product (e.g. a textile print or illustration) to another provider.

- Think about how each other's wider networks intersect but also diverge—leverage the distinct audiences and consider how your business messaging and positioning might be adapted to engage the other in the long term.

- Consider the story behind the collaboration, as this can be used for marketing and publicity.

⊡ DOUBLE DUTY

Reasons to collaborate extend beyond self-promotion and marketing, and could also benefit you in ways such as:

- getting to make a product that you otherwise don't have the capital/funds to invest in yourself (page 104)

- increasing your email subscriber list (page 36); and/or

- gaining media coverage (page 89).

☼ ACTION

Brainstorm: I have always wanted to see my work on/venture into/experiment with...

_____

_____

_____

_____

_____

_____

_____

_____

Potential co-collaborators who share my business' values and aesthetics are:

_____

_____

_____

_____

_____

_____

_____

My goal/s for a collaboration would be:

_____

_____

_____

_____

_____

_____

_____

_____

_____

_____

_____

_____

_____

_____

_____

25

THE POWER OF REWARDING
YOUR CUSTOMERS

Just as important as developing ways to find new
customers and clients, is rewarding the ones that you
have. Depending on your type of business, you could
consider loyalty programs, discounts, samples, gifts, and
special experiences for people who already know, like
and trust you enough to keep coming back.

A QUICK CHAT WITH

A QUICK CHAT WITH

Fatuma & Laurinda Ndenzako

CO-FOUNDERS OF COLLECTIVE CLOSETS

The thing I admire most about sisters Laurinda and Fatuma Ndenzako is the way they have built a fashion retail business on a solid foundation of their values. They don't just want to sell clothing (despite that clothing being responsibly-made, practical, and flattering): everything they do comes back to empowering and centering women and black communities. Following their business over the years, I've also admired the way collaborations have formed a central part of their business model, for both product development and self-promotion.

What's your current vibe re: social media?

Laurinda: Fatuma and I talk about this all the time – our relationship with social media is love-hate. There is a plethora of reasons why, as a small business, we have thrived on platforms like Instagram. When we started, Instagram was still fairly new. So we were able to grow our business quite organically into what it is today. The community building side of social media has been a real positive aspect. The fact that you have the ability to direct message a customer, for instance, who posts wearing our clothing and leave a voice note to say 'you look phenomenal!'. It is amazing to have that instant connection and be able to show that gratitude.

However, over the years, the platforms have changed, and things are different now. When a new app or platform launches, there is FOMO. It's been a little bit difficult for us just to grasp those changes, because they change rapidly. We always try to check in and see if our actual customers are engaging in those new spaces. But for a micro business that has such a small team, we don't have a cohort of staff staying on the pulse with what's happening.

Fatuma: A platform like Instagram is about images, it can get a bit demoralising when you spend time and money on a photo shoot, and people love it and say it's amazing, but they're also just a bit bored because they always want to see something new. The fast turnover of content, and trying to understand how much energy to put into it, is difficult because it can be just so disposable at times.

Right now, we're looking at the content we make and spending a bit more time strategising. We're asking ourselves: how do we find content that uplifts our type of woman? Where do we fit in? What's our voice? What's our point of view? We find ourselves just trying to stay in the present with our social media strategy, just reading the room. And at the same time we're dedicating time, effort and money into SEO and building our email database.

Collective Closets has developed products with fellow small businesses, such as footwear and accessories brand Radical Yes, as well as major cultural institutions including the Australian Centre for the Moving Image (ACMI). What have been some of the surprising or unexpected benefits/outcomes of these collaborations?

Fatuma: Each collaboration brings a different kind of strategy for us — and that can change throughout the process. When we were approached about a collaboration with ACMI, we were thinking about it as a brand exercise — the exposure and reach it would bring to our label. But once we met the team, it was like: these people are amazing, this exhibition stands for so much of what we are about. ACMI have been very generous with their time and offering us opportunities that have now solidified a longer-term partnership.

With Radical Yes, that's also a long standing relationship based on a mutual appreciation of each other's brands, and our store's proximity to each other in North Melbourne. They're like an older, cooler, wiser sister. Every time we collaborate with them, we feel like we're growing and we're getting an insight into what their business looks like and advice from that perspective. It's almost like a mentorship. Also, it is about producing something that we don't have, but also knowing that the customer who was maybe a bit intimidated by our full range really loves it. The collaboration bags we've produced with Radical Yes allow customers to start their journey with us in a small way, and then we find that often they will go on to purchase more.

Laurinda: The big benefit of collaborations is that we are reaching a certain community that maybe we never would have reached before. That in itself is a huge, huge win for us. But what I think these collaborations have done is that they have opened our minds to the scale of what we can do. We always revisit why we started our brand — creativity and celebrating the textiles, amplifying women and black communities. But the possibilities [from a product perspective] are endless.

What advice do you have for people who want to explore collaboration?

Fatuma: For us, it's about how we feel. A collaborative relationship has to feel really good because, a) you have to work with these people, and b) you want to feel like it's mutually beneficial, which it's not always. Sometimes you think the outcome is going be bigger or better. And for us to not be disappointed, we always want there to be a nice feeling of wanting to work with the person or people. There's been a few times where people have asked us to collaborate and we have told them that it doesn't make sense because our customers are not going to relate; and that doesn't really make us feel good. We're happy to walk away. I've also said a few times to potential collaborators: this is what Collective Closets is. So if you're not happy with that, then we're not the right collaborators. I don't want someone to come in and change us.

Laurinda: I think a lot of businesses probably don't tap into collaborations enough, or maybe they're scared they are going to get rejected. To make collaborations a larger part of our brand strategy, we had to undergo a shift in our mindset. If you constantly think of yourself as this small fish in a big pond, then when a bigger business approaches you, you do feel like anything they present to you is just great. 'Exposure? I'll take it.' But when you say, actually, no, we've got a lot to offer you as well, then you don't have to wait to be tapped on the shoulder: You can knock on the door.

Running a business in a partnership with your sister must come with its own challenges — tell us a bit about your experience in this kind of collaboration.

Fatuma: I probably would never build a business with someone that didn't have the same work style or view as me. It's a very intimate relationship. Small business is so up and down. It's great one day, it's bad the other. Early on, even though we would talk every single day, we wouldn't talk about sisterly stuff. Because it was just business, business, business. We've had to work on both sides of our relationship. Sometimes when you're family, you aren't as forgiving. You ask for way more and you don't respect their boundaries as much as someone else that might works for or with you. There are so many pressures in a small business. The work isn't always equal at times. But there's also so much trust there and more understanding. Knowing that someone has my back no matter what makes it such a beautiful experience. It's the most rewarding relationship that you can have because we're building something amazing with someone that we deeply love.

COLLECTIVECLOSETS.COM.AU

Start a podcast

Podcasts can help people develop a connection with an audience that feels quite personal, without being visual. I may not put my face on social media a lot, but I did host a podcast for five years and that's a pretty intimate experience to have with listeners.

When I launched my own podcast in 2014, I was a creative professional juggling my small business alongside my growing family. It was an all-consuming life and I wanted to understand and learn from other people like me who did the same things. It helped that this niche was also the target client for my design business — people who run small businesses. My podcast, The New Normal, had a co-host and we interviewed different guests about their parenting experience. So while I wasn't necessarily talking the whole time about my business or my expertise, allowing myself a platform to help potential clients get to know me worked well for my visibility.

 TIPS AND IDEAS

◆ Being a fan of podcasts helps when you want to create your own. What would you want to listen to? Find a model podcast and listen with the intent of understanding its structure — what works, what doesn't, and what could resonate with your potential audience.

◆ Like a lot of self-promotion activities, questions needs to be asked: who do you want to connect with, and why?

◆ Consider how the structure of your podcast will attract the audience you want to connect with, and how it will reflect the information you share. Common structures for podcasts include Interview podcasts, Series podcasts, Topic-based podcasts.

◆ Consider the schedule you want to release episodes — then stick to it. Irregularity can disengage listeners, but setting expectations can encourage them to subscribe and keep listening.

- If your podcast is conversational, remember that people will be listening to that conversation! Having a plan around what topics to broach and which to avoid is helpful to ensure what you say is of interest to listeners. If you are a podcast guest, for example, being interviewed about your work — have some anecdotes, stories, tips and advice to share.

- Interviews allow diverse voices and insights to merge with your own. Interviewees can also bring their own audiences to your podcast. Interviewing also gives you an opportunity to connect with people you admire or want to learn from.

- Audio quality is important, but you don't need to invest in lots of expensive equipment straight away. Research methods for economically improving audio quality and look out for podcast recording spaces for hire — even your local library might offer this.

- A podcast needn't go forever. Consider launching a short multi-part first series and set audience expectations for the length of the series from the beginning. This is particularly helpful if you are exploring a niche topic or if you want to generate attention for it as a self-contained project.

- If your goal is to make money with your podcast, you might approach it differently than if your goal is to use the podcast as a tool for self-promotion.

- Adding helpful resources and links to your website and other platforms in the 'notes' section will help listeners seek out more information about you and your business.

- Having your own podcast will often lead to being a guest on other podcasts, which can introduce you to new but likeminded audiences.

- If you have ever felt like you wanted to write a book to promote your expertise in your industry, but struggle with the writing part, a podcast could be a good alternative. Consider episodes like chapters, and share your expertise incrementally across multiple episodes.

DOUBLE DUTY

- Record your podcast with videos for upload to a video platform (page 54) or embedding on your website (page 8).

- Use a transcription service to turn podcast content into a blog or newsletter (page 36).

- The content of a podcast could form the basis for a self-published book (page 96).

ACTION

Define the style of your podcast. Consider the structure of podcasts that you really enjoy: what is it about them that makes them feel authentic and reliable? What style would suit the audience you hope to attract?

_____

_____

_____

_____

Define your podcast topic. What is your expertise, or what part of your business do you want to draw attention to?

_____

_____

_____

_____

What can you realistically talk about, at length, that would be of interest to your audience/s?

_____

_____

_____

_____

_____

_____

_____

_____

Sketch out a mind map of your podcast. You can break it down by episode titles, interviewees, parts of the podcast, etc.

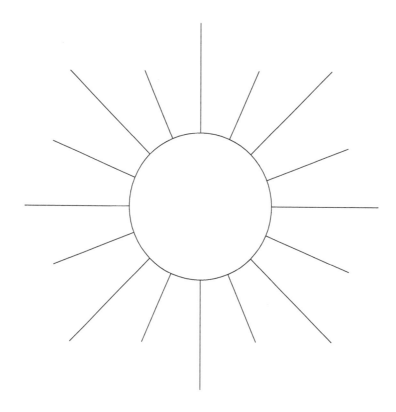

$$\{27\}$$

Send out a press release

This is kind of a retro promotion tactic for free media coverage, but maybe that's why it's so great to do?! Media still exists, in so many forms, and print media adds an extra sparkle of legitimacy to what you do.

Broadcast media is all about that: broadcasting. And if you can insert yourself into a conversation about a particular topic or event, it can increase the visibility of your business.

From taking a major stride or pivot in your business, to devoting time to a project close to your heart, letting media channels know about it can go a long way towards self-promotion.

☀ TIPS AND IDEAS

◆ When deciding who to send a press release to, consider traditional media outlets such as newspapers, magazines, and radio and television stations, as well as online news sites and industry-specific publications, leading industry blogs, and podcasts.

◆ One way to capitalise on a news event for self-promotion is to tie your press release to the event. This can help increase the chances of your press release being picked up by media. For example, if a major event is taking place in your city, tie-in your press release by highlighting how your product or service can be used by locals. Another option is to offer expert commentary on the event, positioning yourself as an authority in your field. Just be sure to make a genuine connection to the event, rather than trying to force it.

◆ Have your content at the ready! A link to a cloud-based storage system that features swipe copy (e.g. bios, press release), high-quality imagery, and details about your digital real estate makes it easy for media outlets to quickly and correctly promote your story.

- Consider crafting your pitch to an individual journalist who works in an industry niche for several publications. Developing relationships with journalists may take time, but can be well worth the effort. Do your research, and be concise and compelling in your outreach. (Some ego-stroking goes a long way, too!).

- Don't forget to reach out to places that have promoted you in the past when you have something new to share.

- Write for the attention span you're likely to encounter. Keep it short and to the point, generally no more than one page.

- Use a clear and attention-grabbing headline, and include all of the important information in the first paragraph. The takeaway should be crystal clear.

- Use a professional tone and avoid hype or exaggeration (unless that's what you're going for in a tongue-in-cheek way!), but don't be afraid to include your brand's tone of voice.

- Use quotes from key players or experts to add credibility and interest. It's helpful if this adds information or supports the project or the key takeaway.

- It helps if your 'news' is timely — consider how it could link in with current cultural conversations, holidays, events or recognised days.

- Provide contact information for follow-up questions.

- Track the open rate of your press release by sending it through an newsletter platform, rather than as an attachment in an email.

- Don't be discouraged if you don't hear back right away, or at all. A short follow-up message that highlights the key points of your original press release (and the reasons why your product/service is ideal for their audiencen) is fine, especially if you are establishing a relationship with a particular journalist or editor.

- Remember that you want to write about your business in third person. Visualise how it might sound if you were reading it in a magazine or news platform.

- Send a test to yourself, and a trusted friend or colleague — it's an easy way to test links, and pick up details you might not otherwise have noticed.

- Proofread, proofread, proofread!

⊞ DOUBLE DUTY

- ◆ A press release can be repurposed into a newsletter or blog post (page 36).
- ◆ Share a press release (and any subsequent media coverage!) with your retailers (page 32).

☼ ACTION

Make a list of publications that you think your ideal customer would read, and that your product or service aligns to. Most publications (both digital and print) have a niche and understanding that niche is key to being featured. List some here:

Publication name	Distribution schedule	Contact name and email address

Now, write your press release:

- ☐ Start with a clear and attention-grabbing headline that summarises the main point of your press release.

- ☐ Write a brief introduction that provides some context for the information you're presenting. Include the most important information in the first paragraph: who, what, when, where, and why.

- ☐ Source a quote or two from someone involved in your project (it could even be yourself!) to add credibility and interest.

- ☐ Provide additional details in subsequent paragraphs, but keep the press release concise and to the point.

- ☐ Include contact information for follow-up questions, and a link to a folder of images (at high resolution) and other relevant information.

⚡

People who offer opportunities are
more likely to invest in you if they can
see you're investing in yourself through
active self-promotion.

☐ NOT APPLICABLE   ☐ SOMETHING TO CONSIDER   ☐ YES, DO IT!

Host a workshop or demonstration

Workshops and demonstrations are a great way to build an audience of invested customers and clients. And while there might be a fear that 'DIY' will impact the saleability of your key service or product, the strategy behind what you offer can easily mitigate concerns.

In some ways, a DIY workshop can either prepare potential clients for working with you, or elevate your services or products in your customer's mind beyond what they themselves can achieve. Plus, customers or clients who get the opportunity to like, know and trust you via an intimate workshop setting are likely to become advocates for your brand and increase your reach via word-of-mouth.

If making connections with customers beyond a quick transaction is important to you, a workshop can be a great way to strengthen that tie. There are also many cross-promotion opportunities to be harnessed if your workshop is part of a festival, showcase or collaboration, and lots of ways that the content of a workshop can be repurposed for other promotion and income streams.

⌖ TIPS AND IDEAS

- ◆ Collaborative workshops are great for audience cross-promotion and an opportunity to expand your skills and creativity. Think a florist collaborating with a watercolour artist on a botanical painting workshop, or a graphic designer and a copywriter collaborating on a content-marketing workshop.

- ◆ Show people how to begin in your medium with an easy project that teaches basic skills. Choose something that is easily repeatable in a class setting or at home.

- ◆ Workshops needn't be presented in person. Pre-recorded lessons, self-guided eBooks, and online workshops are all valid alternatives to in-person sessions and can broaden the reach, scale, and longevity of your workshop idea.

◆ Consider holding a workshop or demonstration as a festival satellite event. The festival will likely promote your workshop and business in print media, digital marketing, and other ways. Festivals run by not-for-profit organisations or government bodies are usually bootstrapped, so if you want to leverage them for extra promotion, it helps to make it easy for them. Have some great images and snappy text on hand, and if you're confident, put your hand up for media opportunities such as radio or news features.

▯▯ DOUBLE DUTY

◆ Workshops could be recorded and uploaded to Youtube as evergreen video content (page 93).

◆ List your workshops on local event listing websites or ticketing marketplaces — these websites often offer the ability to embed their booking processor or widget into your own website, making purchase and management of workshop bookings simple for you and the attendee. These websites often rank highly on search engines and their internal algorithms will serve your workshop to people searching within a defined geographic area or in a similar category.

◆ If a class proves popular, start a waiting list. This could be the basis of your email newsletter (page 36).

◆ Develop a step-by-step guide to an activity as a lead magnet that encourages people to join your mailing list (page 12).

◆ Creating workshop content can help you to refine your own systems and processes.

◆ Presenting a workshop can build the courage and confidence for other self-promotion opportunities such as public speaking at events (page 45).

☼ ACTION

A basic skill that I could teach or demonstrate that is related to my business is:

_____

_____

_____

To host this workshop I will need:

_____

_____

_____

_____

_____

Possible dates for an in-person workshop (consider local festivals, activities, conferences etc related to your industry or customer base):

_____

_____

_____

_____

_____

Brainstorm potential ideas for a collaborative workshop:

_____

_____

_____

_____

_____

To record this workshop for online delivery I will need:

_____

_____

_____

_____

_____

29

Self-publish a book

Writing or publishing a book is something many people aspire to do in their lifetime. Not only because it can be a fulfilling creative endeavour, but because it can also establish credibility and promote you and your work to a wide audience.

Why did I start writing and publishing books? In the early days, it's because I wanted to be known as a book designer, and to promote my side business, a networking group for creative women. (Spoiler alert, people now hire me to design their self-published books. Plus, the book raised the profile of the group from one that existed locally, to having multiple national locations!).

The type of book you produce can affect the outcome of this promotion tool. If your strategy is to cement your legacy in your industry, a collection of your work or writing across your career might be appropriate. If you want to promote yourself as a thought leader, coach, or mentor, a book can also serve as a powerful marketing tool and open up new opportunities for speaking engagements, clients, consulting projects, and other forms of professional recognition.

 TIPS AND IDEAS

◆ Be clear on your goals for writing a book. Is it to raise your profile within your industry? Is it to generate customers and clients for a particular service that you offer? Is it to establish your expertise in your field? Is it a visual archive of your work to date? Is it to offer advice and guidance to those in your industry who are up-and-coming? Is it a personal creative project? Is it to have a product that generates revenue? Your answer might be one or many of the above!

• While getting a deal with a traditional publisher is competitive, in recent years self-publishing a high-quality book has become a more accessible option for aspiring writers and small business owners.

- If you decide to self-publish, you have complete control over the content, design, and distribution. This means you can create the book you want, without having to compromise your vision to meet the requirements of a traditional publisher. You also have the flexibility to choose your own publishing timeline and marketing strategy (which could include so many of the ideas you're reading about here!).

- By publishing a book with an ISBN (International Standard Book Number) and barcode, your book will then be listed in databases that are used by booksellers to search for books and place orders. ISBNs are used by libraries, booksellers, and distributors to identify and order books. If you plan to sell your book through any retail outlet, you will need to obtain an ISBN for your book.

- Investing in a professional design for your book will help, as bookstores will potentially stock a self-published title if it is of a comparable quality and standard to professionally published books.

- Printing costs for a book vary based on the size, length, style, and specifications of a book. A black and white paperback novel will be more economic to print than a full-colour hardcover book with high-quality photos or illustrations.

- Printing a large number of books at once can bring down the unit cost per book, as fixed costs are spread out over a larger number of books. This usually means a smaller production cost per book as a fraction of the book's retail price. However, it's important to keep in mind that printing a large number of books can also lead to large shipping and storage costs.

- You can avoid printing a large number of books at once by using a print-on-demand (POD) platform. POD books are printed only when they are ordered — and they can be ordered in smaller batches, a few as one copy. This can be a cost-effective way to self-publish, especially if you are unsure of how many copies you will sell, and can be an effective way to test the popularity of a book before investing in a larger print run.

- A book distributor is a company that helps get books into the hands of retailers and libraries. They take orders, deliver the product, and handle invoicing and payments for the books that are sold for a commission on the book's retail price. Through a distributor, self-published authors can get their books into more stores and reach a wider audience than they might be able to on their own.

- Printed books have an undeniable physical presence. Not all books will translate to digital eBooks or audiobooks, but it's useful to consider how these formats can expand the reach of your book's content.

☐ NOT APPLICABLE   ☐ SOMETHING TO CONSIDER   ☐ YES, DO IT!

- Publishing your book as an eBook allows you to include interactive features, such as hyperlinks, videos and audio clips, to enhance the reader experience. An experienced eBook designer or conversion service will ensure that your book is formatted correctly for digital devices, including smartphones, tablets, and e-readers.

- Recording an audiobook can be a time-consuming and expensive process, but it can also be a valuable investment, especially if it suits the content, your target audience, or your overarching self-promotion strategy.

- Editors, designers, and printers are often noted on the copyright page of a book. This can be a good place to find professionals that other authors you admire have worked with.

- Self-publishing consultants, book coaches, and ghost writers exist to help you through the stages of writing a book if you don't know where to begin.

- Generally, a book needs two types of editing. Copy editing focuses on the details of the writing, such as grammar, punctuation, and spelling. This process ensures that the writing is clear, concise, and consistent. Structural editing focuses on the overall structure and organisation of the writing. It considers the flow of the writing, the pacing, and the overall effectiveness of the content. A professional book editor can suggest changes to the structure or order of your book's content, as well as provide feedback on the overall message and tone of the writing. Both types of editing are important in ensuring the quality of a book, but they focus on different aspects of the writing process. You may find an editor with both copy editing and structural editing skills, or choose to use different professionals for each part of the writing process.

- While the financial benefit of having a book might be a drawcard, most often it's the promotional aspect of having a book to your name that will benefit you the most. Only in rare cases does a book sell enough copies to justify the time and effort an author will put in — and that's true for self-publishers and traditional publishers alike.

▣▣ DOUBLE DUTY

- You can create video content in support of the book (such as book trailers, Q&As, and interviews) — see page 54 for more.
- Your book can be a gateway to presentations, talks, or workshops at festivals or conferences (page 42, 45 and 93).
- The topics covered in your book can be content for a podcast (page 85), or create interview opportunities (page 89).

ACTION

What are your goals for writing a book?

1 _____

2 _____

3 _____

What is your expertise, or what part of your business do you want to draw attention to?

_____

_____

_____

_____

_____

What can you realistically write about, at length, that would be of interest to your audience/s?

_____

_____

_____

_____

_____

_____

_____

Who is on your team?

☐ Structural editor   ☐ Proofreader

☐ Copyeditor   ☐ Printer

☐ Designer   ☐ Distributor

Sketch out a mind map of your book. You can break it down by topics, chapter titles, activities, sections, etc.

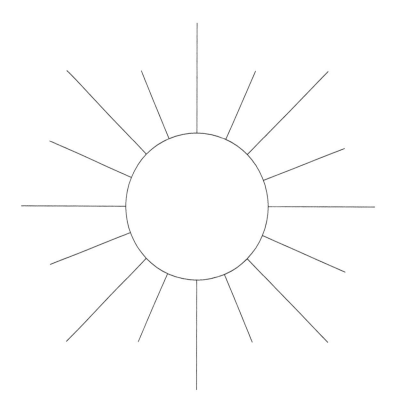

30

THE POWER OF MERCHANDISE

Like printed collateral, tactile items that reflect the values and qualities of your business can elicit a strong mental and emotional link between you, your work, and your business. It's not just musicians and sports teams who have a monopoly on merchandise. Any business can make something that customers and clients want to receive and hang on to. I'm not talking about tacky, poorly made, your-logo-everywhere 'swag'. Consider how the scope of your business' visual identity (i.e, its logo) can be expanded to create impactful merchandise that customers are proud to wear and use. Then, apply your knowledge of your ideal customer or client to develop merchandise to suit.

A QUICK CHAT WITH

Anna Featherstone

WRITER AND AUTHOR

I've found that people who choose to self-publish a book are a collegial bunch. This is probably because the process of publishing a book without the scaffolding of a traditional publishing house can be fraught. I first met Anna when she was writing *Look — It's Your Book!*, her in-depth guide to self-publishing a non-fiction book. Anna interviewed me in her book about book cover design (and then I ended up designing the book's cover!). She's a fount of knowledge for all things writing, self-publishing, and book and author marketing.

What's your current vibe re: social media?

There are gorgeous glimmers of connection, opportunity, sheer delight and some fab insights into people and the world, but the never ending gush of it can also drown time, focus, usefulness and visibility. Bigger picture… there is so much power concentrated in the hands/servers of so few, it makes individuals, businesses and society vulnerable whether from escalating prices for ads, platform changes, misinformation or the price we pay with our attention. So my vibe… hopeful but wary.

What are some activities that you recommend writers do to increase their visibility outside of social media?

It depends on the type of book but you could start by attending author talks, writers festivals and book launches to immerse yourself in, show support to, as well as learn from the writing community. Join or start a writing group too so you can have and be part of a support network. Start talking about your book early, share your advance information/book sell sheet far and wide, get some PR rolling and offer to do talks to various groups and clubs. Collaborate with other individuals and businesses on a promotion, go old school with a magnetic sign on your car, send out and gift review copies to key people to get the word-of-mouth ball rolling… there's so much you can do — and will need to do! But most important of all: write and publish a great book — and make sure it has a fab cover.

How might an author's visibility strategy differ depending on the kind of book they are publishing, for example, a children's book versus a non-fiction business book, versus a novel, versus a 'coffee table' book.

It varies hugely as it's all about where your audience is, what they're into and what problem you're solving for them. Your book might offer entertainment, an escape, inspiration or facts, but no book is of interest to 'everyone'. Narrow your target audience and learn as much about them as you can so you can go deep on your promotion to them. It might mean you create and promote an event, run a competition, do a pop up stall at a market, work with a store (and it doesn't have to be a bookstore) to design a killer window display, sponsor an event, get yourself on a conference panel, design cool merchandise as part of your brand extension, hire a 'name' to narrate the audiobook version or use simple PR techniques to boost your visibility. It's all about momentum, one thing leads to another, but if you sit on your hands because you don't want to put yourself out there, your book won't reach readers.

What are some of the promotion activities you have undertaken to promote your own books that aren't just posting about them on social media?

Some of the key things I do is write and place stories with a variety of media plus pitch angles to radio producers to secure interviews. I send my book sell sheets far and wide and do presentations and workshops for all sorts of organisations from libraries to small business groups. I'm into collaborations too, such as with other authors on the initiative boldauthors.com which helps us all expand our presence while still contributing to the writing community. You also need a professional website with email collection capabilities. It's the only platform you can truly control.

The promotion activities for me really begin when, as I'm writing the books, I think about who I can interview to expand the reach and quality of the book. I also plan the manuscript so it naturally includes media opportunities—such as interviewing interesting experts and people in different regions so it makes the book PR-able and relevant in different states. I live and breathe the philosophy that if you care enough about a topic or character to write a book, you need to care enough about getting it to readers—that means talking about it, marketing it and giving it your all.

ANNAFEATHERSTONE.COM
BOLDAUTHORS.COM

31

Start a self-initiated project

Self-initiated projects (SIPs) have been paramount to my career and success as a designer. My books, my podcast, and my time hosting networking events for the creative community contributed significantly to the visibility of me and my business, helped me meet tons of people (many of whom have become clients and collaborators), and developed my professional skill set.

An SIP can be a great way to showcase your skills in a particular area, especially if it's the type of work you want to be paid for.

By taking the initiative to create something on your own, you demonstrate passion and commitment to your craft, explore new ideas and push yourself creatively. SIPs can also be a way to combat burnout by allowing for creative exploration and experimentation without the pressure of client demands. By taking on a project that is purely for personal fulfillment, you can reignite passion for your craft and gain a new sense of motivation and inspiration.

And remember, if a creative experiment doesn't work out, at least you can learn from the experience and use the knowledge you gained to inform your future projects. SIPs can be a feature of a portfolio as an example of your process and creative explorations.

TIPS AND IDEAS

- ◆ Initiate a project in response to a theme set out by a local festival, event or cultural conversation. By setting parameters for your project, you can push yourself creatively and develop new skills. Remember, a self-initiated project can be a great way to showcase your abilities and gain experience in an area you want to be paid for.

- ◆ Funding a self-initiated project can be one barrier to getting it out into the world. You can use your own money, crowdfund, or apply for grants or sponsorship. But if none of those options are available, often the shape of the idea must change. You should consider the costs not sunk, but invested.

- SIPs can provide a space to try and to fail, without consequences that could cost you a client or a job. You might even consider taking your audience along for the journey, documenting your experiments and the results of your project.

- SIPs can be a key part of a career pivot, especially if you want to leverage any publicity that you already have through a business or work you have done in the past.

- A creative challenge with strict parameters, such as a commitment to doing something every day for a set period of time, or to using only certain materials, colours or formats, can be both an SIP and something that creates content for a newsletter or press release.

- SIPs could take the form of a brief you set yourself to demonstrate the skills you have so that a potential client can recognise your abilities.

🔋🔋 DOUBLE DUTY

- If your SIP is a self-published book or a collaboration with a fellow creative, these can come with other promotional benefits (pages 78 and 96).

- Consider how your SIP can aid your self-promotion:
  - Have a launch (page 45)
  - Display it publicly
  - Send out a press release (page 89)
  - Make it a feature of your website (page 8)
  - Make it into a series
  - Contact potential collaborators using the project as an example (page 78)
  - Create it as part of a widely-promoted festival or event.

☀ ACTION

What have you always wanted to create but time/funds/experience was a barrier?

_____

_____

_____

□ NOT APPLICABLE   □ SOMETHING TO CONSIDER   □ YES, DO IT!

Describe the project and how it relates to the work or business you ultimately want to do:

_____

_____

_____

_____

_____

_____

If you spend your days thinking 'I'd rather be doing X', what's the minimum you need to do to get started?

☐ Take a class

☐ Buy materials

☐ Buy a domain name

☐ Contact a supplier

☐ Write a list of pros

☐ Dedicate a sum of money to the idea

☐ Contact a potential collaborator

☐ Workshop the idea with a mate or colleague

Set some parameters around your project:

A scaled back version of the project looks like...

_____

An all-in version of the project looks like...

_____

I will dedicate _____ hours to this project every _____

I will finish by _____

I will be held accountable by _____

32

Enter awards

It's easy to understand why awards are a big draw for creatives. The lights! The kudos! The glory! When your sense of purpose is tied to your creative output, an award can feel great.

Winning an award can provide significant exposure for a business. It can help attract the attention of potential clients, collaborators, and industry experts, which can lead to new projects and collaborations.

But you know what? Not everyone wins awards. In fact, sometimes, in the creative industries, it feels like the same people win awards over and over again. It can feel demoralising to consistently feel under-recognised for your work.

I'm here to tell you: keep entering.

Simply entering awards can be beneficial for your career. It provides an opportunity to showcase your work and get it in front of industry experts and potential clients — after all, by entering an award, your work has likely been seen, discussed, and remembered. That visibility can lead to some surprising results, even without the glory of a big win.

 TIPS AND IDEAS

◆ Behind the scenes, the organisation and categorisation of awards entries, and the process by which the judges come to their decisions, is often hard to discern. I've been on judging panels where the selection process is highly subjective, or where the shortlisting of entries is completely out of the judges hands. You never know when you came *this close* to winning. And often, in situations where judges work together to select winners, there are judges who advocate hard for an entry that just doesn't receive enough support to claim the victory. Despite all this, by entering, your work can be seen and connect with people — people with status in an industry.

- Investigate who is on the judging panel at the awards of your choice. Once the awards are over and the judges no longer feel a conflict of interest, try approaching a judge for feedback or insight into your work.

- Don't overlook smaller awards or international awards.

- Entering (but not winning) awards also forces you to evaluate your work and identify areas where you can improve, adapt, or eschew the awards completely. Some awards have a very narrow vision of what is considered 'worthy'! The act of entering awards can help you build confidence in your own style, and motivate you to continue creating new work.

🔋 DOUBLE DUTY

- Awards submission info can force you to write about a project and highlight some of its most successful angles and outcomes. This can form the basis of website or newsletter content, such as a case study (pages 8 and 36).

- Awards often culminate in an industry event which is a great place to meet peers and potential clients (page 42).

- You might also want to have professional photos taken of the work which can be reused on your website (page 8), on Pinterest (page 63), or in a press release (page 89).

☀ ACTION

Research awards in your industry. Start with industry peers (it's definitely something many people use as a promotional opportunity!) and also look at associations and guilds.

Use the table on the following page to list award opening and closing dates, submission requirements, and entry fees.

SELF-PROMOTION WITHOUT SOCIAL MEDIA

Award name	Opening date	Closing date	Submission requirements	Entry fee

⚡

It bears repeating:
Comparison is the thief of joy.
You are you. Don't compare someone else's
numbers/likes/follows/awards/success
to your own.

33

THE POWER OF PROMOTING OTHERS

When you run a small business, a supportive and kind community of peers, customers and clients is essential. As difficult as it can be some days to compare our own shortcomings with others' successes, alongside every 'success story' is a tale or two of failure, second-guessing, privilege or shaky foundations that you will never hear. The higher ground is to always choose community over competition. This is something I have learned, sometimes the hard way, at various points in my business.

Sharing and promoting the work of others can help you to build credibility and trust with your audience, but when you support and promote other businesses, you create a sense of community and collaboration. People rarely ignore (or forget) genuine compliments. The key is to always fold kindness, empathy, and care into the recipe of how you promote yourself.

Many of the suggestions for self-promotion in this book can incorporate kindness towards others. Whether you are promoting the work of others in a newsletter, on a podcast, at an event, or in conversation, planting seeds of kindness along your business journey is sure to bear fruit for your own business ventures.

Conclusion

When I decided to leave the safety of a salaried income and become self-employed, my mantra was: 'nothing ventured, nothing gained'. Even if I tried and failed, I would learn something about myself, my clients, and my business model.

I encourage you to approach self-promotion outside of social media with a similar mindset. Begin. Experiment. Tweak.

Whatever avenues for self-promotion and visibility you choose to pursue, there are a few other things to note:

YOU STILL NEED TO SHOW UP

While you might not feel the pressure to create new content every day like we do on social media, some of these strategies will only work in the long term if you continue to show up for your audience on a consistent schedule. Set realistic expectations for your audience around how often they will receive your newsletter or hear a new podcast episode. Maybe you'll build up to the launch of a meaty self-initiated project and then rest for a year while it does its thing in the world.

Some of these strategies are 'set and forget', some will take effort at the beginning and then only light maintenance as time goes on. Some require lots of focus to set up, but if you're strategic, they are replicable and low-maintenance.

WORD-OF-MOUTH IS POWERFUL (AND MORE EFFECTIVE OFF SOCIAL MEDIA)

Word-of-mouth is a powerful and important promotion tool. The thing is, while there are things you can do to generate word-of-mouth, you can't make it happen directly. It's out of your control. But we do know the ingredients of this age-old recipe: a good experience with a business (or person) that we know, like and trust. That, and visibility.

MEASURE YOUR SUCCESS

I love seeing the connection between a self-promotion activity that I pursued and the path that led a client or customer to my door. Sometimes it's not always obvious, and other times, clients can't wait to tell me where they first found my work. It's a lovely feeling to have impacted someone in a small way, and then for that person to trust me enough to help them in their journey. I encourage you to investigate how your clients and customers have come to find you. The results of these inquiries (be they formal, like a survey question, or through more casual means like a conversation) can do so much to help you strategise your self-promotion activities.

YOU DON'T HAVE TO DO IT ALL!

33 ways to promote your business is a lot of ways! Remember: they are suggestions. You don't have to (and likely cannot) do them all. Choose avenues that are realistic for your time, budget, and energy. You still need to work *in* your business, after all.

There are so many great tools and resources out there to help make your self-promotion plans into reality. I've compiled an evolving list of resources I use, like or recommend for the activities in this book. You can find them via **www.creativemindshq.com/spwsm** (enter the password **spwsm** to access the list).

SELF-PROMOTION GOAL SETTING

Things to tackle / edit / change now:

1 _____

2 _____

3 _____

Activities to explore / research more:

1 _____

2 _____

3 _____

Long-term goals:

1 _____

2 _____

3 _____

In the next 3 months, I will:

_____

_____

_____

_____

By this time next year, I will have:

_____

_____

_____

_____

Thanks

A book like this comes together only through the support and effort of a fantastic team. Thank you to Emily Rolfe for her expert editing and soundboarding; Ben Aitchison at Paradigm Print Media for his patience and print management; my dad, Peter Donoughue, for his keen proofreading eyes; and Sonja Jeffrey and the team at Books At Manic for distribution and promotion with a smile. Thank you to my wonderful retailers — I still get such a thrill seeing my books in the wild. Big thanks to Alicia Cohen for her publishing advice (and checklists). Shout out to Jade Roberts, Pip Tweed, Angela D'Alton and Renee Baker for our fruitful conversations about business, marketing, self-promotion, self-employment, and the ideas in this book — they are a salve. Caz Butler, Bec Smith, and Claire Deane: your feedback was so helpful and helped make it better than I thought it could be. Special thanks to Elizabeth Bull, Anna Featherstone, Jenna Hipgrave, Yvonne Meng, Fatuma Ndenzako, Laurinda Ndenzako and Jeremy Wortsman for the experience and wisdom they shared — I deeply admire the businesses you lead and impact you have on those around you. To my fantastic clients who informed many of the topics, tips and ideas covered in this book — thank you for our conversations and for trusting me to help elevate your businesses. Huge hugs to my extended family, friends, and my two excellent kiddos — I'm so lucky to have you in my life. And last but very definitely not least, thank you to Patrick McCabe for your unwavering encouragement and support. Chip chip chip.

About the author

Tess McCabe has two decades of experience as a graphic and website designer.

Her clients are primarily small businesses and companies of one. They have enjoyed working with her not only for her creative, clear, and concept-driven design work but for her reliability, efficiency, critical-thinking skills, and friendly demeanour.

Tess was the director and president of Creative Women's Circle, a national association that supports, champions and connects women working in creative industries and running their own businesses, from 2009–2018. She was a judge for Frankie Magazine's Good Stuff Awards from 2016–2021, and for the Australian Graphic Design Awards in 2021. Her podcast, *The New Normal,* ran from 2014 to 2020. She has also spoken at Creative Mornings and given talks and presentations for many other organisations, institutions, and podcasts.

You can find Tess' books in design shops, galleries, bookstores, online retailers, and at the Creative Minds website. Tess also sends a monthly newsletter for self-employed business owners called Sylloge, offering tips and advice for running a creative business, with links to podcasts, articles and other internet ephemera that creative minds like you might enjoy. Subscribe at **creativemindshq.com/sylloge**.

BOOKS BY TESS McCABE

- *Graphic Design Speak: Tips, Advice and Jargon Defined for Non-Graphic Designers*
- *Conversations with Creative Women: Volumes 1–3*
- *DIY SEO: How to Optimise Your Website to Get More Clients, Customers, and Sales*

FIND TESS ONLINE

- tessmccabe.com.au

SELF-PROMOTION WITHOUT SOCIAL MEDIA

About Creative Minds

Creative Minds exists to provide practical advice and oodles of inspiration for creative business owners. Our books and resources provide actionable information and insights to support you to create an impactful business that's sustainable in the long term.

VISIT US ONLINE

- creativemindshq.com

Notes/thoughts/ideas:

Printed in the USA
CPSIA information can be obtained
at www.ICGtesting.com
LVHW061317211123
764504LV00021BA/620

9 780994 627391